ERASING THE STIGMA OF MENTAL ILLNESS THROUGH AWARENESS

Managing Unwanted Thoughts, Feelings and Actions Workbook

A TOOLBOX of REPRODUCIBLE ASSESSMENTS and ACTIVITIES for Facilitators

Ester R.A. Leutenberg
and John J. Liptak, EdD

WholePerson
Mental Health & Wellness
publisher of therapy, counseling, and self-help resources

Whole Person Associates
101 West 2nd Street, Suite 203
Duluth, MN 55802

800-247-6789

Books@WholePerson.com
WholePerson.com

Managing Unwanted Thoughts, Feelings and Actions Workbook
A Toolbox of Reproducible Assessments and Activities for Facilitators.

Printed in the United States of America

10 9 8 7 6 5 4 3 2 1

Editorial Director: Carlene Sippola
Art Director: Joy Morgan Dey
Assistant Art Director: Mathew Pawlak

Library of Congress Control Number: 2014957801
ISBN: 978-157025-326-3

Using the *Managing Unwanted Thoughts, Feelings and Actions* Workbook

People who encounter unwanted thoughts, feelings and actions face frightening experiences. They may have a difficult time distinguishing between what is real and what is not real. They usually regret what they thought and felt, and/or how they acted. They find that often this interferes with their work, school, family relationships, and interactions with friends and people in their community. Unwanted thoughts, feelings and actions can cause confusion, be difficult to deal with, and disrupt any setting.

Mental health issues contribute to unwanted thoughts, feelings and actions. When adults experience these symptoms, they are typically challenged by being and remaining in touch with reality. They have difficulty coping with the stressors and demands of their daily lives.

How Do Unwanted Thoughts, Feelings and Actions Issues Manifest Themselves?

Because there are so many bizarre ways these feelings can manifest themselves, disturbances can be very difficult to identify and manage. It is critical to be aware of, to understand, and to acknowledge how symptoms are commonly experienced. Although most or all symptoms to do not have to be present, those that are present will typically cause significant distress and/or impairment in daily functioning.
Listed below are some possible symptoms:

- Agitation
- Cold manner
- Confused thoughts
- Dangerous actions
- Delusions
- Detached from others
- Difficulties in the workplace
- Disinterest in maintaining personal hygiene
- Disorganized speech
- Feelings of entrapment
- Flat affect
- Forgetfulness
- Hallucinations
- Inability to understand and accept reality
- Inability to communicate well with others
- Inability to express emotions
- Inability to make good decisions and judgments
- Inability to think clearly and rationally
- Inappropriate behavior
- Incoherent speech
- Increased drug/alcohol use
- Intense anxiety
- Loss of appetite
- Loss of interest in everyday activities
- Loss of touch with reality
- Mood swings
- Problems in school
- Problems maintaining relationships
- Rigid actions
- Strange actions
- Suicidal thoughts
- Unusual movements
- Withdrawal from others socially

Our goal for this workbook is NOT to diagnose mental illness, or even for the facilitator to make such a diagnosis from this workbook's content. Our goal is to touch on some of the symptoms and possibilities, create realizations, and provide coping methods which will help people to go forward and perhaps consider the possibility of the need for medications and therapy. Our goal is also to help participants recognize that other people have the same issues, that no shame is connected to them, and mental health issues of any degree are not to be stigmatized nor should anyone feel like a victim of stereotyping. In this workbook, we are using the phrase mental health issues to include all types of unwanted thoughts, feelings and actions issues, from having a few problems to a serious mental illness.

Sources of Unwanted Thoughts, Feelings and Actions Issues

As with many different types of psychological problems, the origin of these unwanted thoughts, feelings and actions issues are difficult to pinpoint. Because of their complex nature, these issues are often brought on by one or a variety of these sources:

Genetics and Biology

Psychotic disturbances often run in families and thus researchers believe that they are inherited, but that is not the only cause. A complete medical and psychological history should be collected by a medical professional to identify family members who may also have experienced disturbances with unwanted thoughts, feelings and actions.

Brain Chemistry

The structure and functioning of the brain has been shown to have an effect on the incidence of psychotic disturbances. Chemicals in the brain (neurotransmitters) that communicate between neurons, also seem to play a role. In addition, the structure of the brain found in healthy individuals is different from that of people who experience disturbances with unwanted thoughts, feelings and actions. An examination to explore the structure and functioning of the brain should be conducted by a medical professional.

Life Events

An inability to cope with major stressors can be a factor in disturbances in thoughts, feelings and actions. Some of the major stressors might include traumatic shock or abuse. An examination of the person's life events that may be causing unwanted thoughts, feelings and actions needs to be conducted by a medical professional.

Medical Conditions

Disturbances with unwanted thoughts, feelings and actions are more likely to occur in people with poor medical health in general, or those who suffer from an existing psychological problem. A medical history can reveal conditions that might induce problems in thoughts, feelings and actions, and should be examined by a medical professional.

Substances

A history of problematic drinking, tobacco, marijuana or other drug use has been associated with the development of disturbances with unwanted thoughts, feelings and actions. A history of a person's drug, tobacco and alcohol use should be examined by a medical professional.

How the *Managing Unwanted Thoughts, Feelings and Actions Workbook* Can Help

People experience many different types of problems related to unwanted thoughts, feelings and actions. The assessments and activities in this workbook are designed to provide facilitators with a wide variety of tools to use in helping people manage their lives more effectively. Many choices for self-exploration are provided for facilitators to determine which tools best suit the unique needs of their clients.

The purpose of this workbook is to provide a user-friendly guide to short-term assessments and activities to help people manage their unwanted thoughts, feelings and actions, and experience a greater sense of well-being. In addition, this workbook is designed to help provide facilitators and participants with tools and information needed to overcome the stigma attached to issues of unwanted thoughts, feelings and actions.

In order to help participants deal successfully with unwanted thoughts, feelings and action issues, facilitators need to have a variety of assessments and activities to help their participants open-up and begin to feel they can manage the symptoms of their unwanted thoughts, feelings and actions and realize that they are not alone. *The Managing Unwanted Thoughts, Feelings and Actions Workbook* provides assessments and self-guided activities to help participants understand the intensity of their issues and how they can lead a more effective life.

When to Worry?

Disturbances in unwanted thoughts, feelings and actions are difficult to manage because they blur the line between what is real and what is not real. The good news is that people can develop the skills needed to manage the symptoms and progress forward to begin enjoying life more. Unwanted thoughts, feelings and actions that accompany many of the mental health issues that people deal with daily can be a very frightening way to live. **People who experience these issues over time are at risk of having a serious mental illness and need to seek a medical professional.**

Suicide Warning!

People who experience severe bouts of unwanted thoughts, feelings and actions are often at risk for suicide. Sometimes they can become irrational and think that the only way to escape the pain is to attempt suicide. Remember to take any talk about suicide or suicidal acts very seriously.

Signs of suicidal thoughts:

- Withdrawing from family, friends, and activities of interest in the past
- Increasing use of harmful substances
- Giving away possessions
- Expressing severe hopelessness about the future
- Making a plan for dying by suicide
- Calling or visiting people to say goodbye
- Getting legal affairs in order
- Engaging in reckless actions
- Talking about killing or harming self
- Expressing feelings of being trapped with no way out
- Purchasing a weapon

Serious Mental Illness

If participants have a serious mental illness, they need to do much more than complete the assessments, activities and exercises contained in this workbook. They need to be taken seriously and facilitators can take an active role in their finding help immediately. All disturbances of thoughts, feelings and actions need to be thoroughly evaluated by a medical professional, and then treated with an appropriate combination of medication and group and/or individual therapy.

Format of the *Managing Unwanted Thoughts, Feelings and Actions Workbook*

The *Managing Unwanted Thoughts, Feelings and Actions Workbook* is designed to be used either independently or as part of an established mental health issue program. You may administer any of the assessments and the guided self-exploration activities to an individual or a group with whom you are working, and you may administer any of the assessments and activities over one or more days. Feel free to pick and choose those that best fit the outcomes you desire. The purpose of this workbook is to provide facilitators who work with individuals and groups who may be experiencing unwanted thoughts, feelings and actions issues with a series of reproducible activities that can used to supplement their work with participants. Because these activity pages are reproducible, they can be photocopied as is, or you may adapt them by whiting out and writing in your own changes to suit the need of each group, and then using that page as your master to be photocopied for each participant.

Assessments

Assessments establish a behavioral baseline from which facilitators and participants can gauge progress toward identified goals. This workbook will supplement a facilitator's work by providing assessments designed to measure behavioral baselines for measuring client change. In order to do so, assessments with scoring directions and interpretation materials begin each chapter. The authors recommend that you begin presenting each topic by asking participants to complete the assessment. Facilitators can choose one or more, or all of the activities relevant to their participants' specific needs and concerns.

Each of the awareness modules contained in this workbook begin with an assessment for these purposes:

- Help facilitators to develop a numerical baseline of behavior, attitude and personality characteristics before they begin their plan of treatment.
- Help participants gather valuable information about themselves.
- Help facilitators in the measurement of change over time.
- Use as pre-tests and post-tests to measure changes in behavior, attitude, and personality.
- Help facilitators identify patterns that negatively affect each participant.
- Prompt insight and behavioral change.
- Assist participants to feel a part of the treatment planning process.
- Provide participants with a starting point to begin to learn more about themselves, their strengths and their limitations.

Assessments are a great aid in developing plans for effective change. Be aware of the following when administering, scoring, and interpreting the assessments in this workbook:

- The purpose of these assessments is not to pigeonhole people, but to allow them to explore various elements of themselves and their situations.
- This book contains self-assessments and not tests. Traditional tests measure knowledge or right or wrong responses. For the assessments provided in this workbook, remind participants that there are no right or wrong answers. These assessments ask only for opinions, self-observations or attitudes.
- The assessments in this workbook have face value, but have not been formally normed for validity and reliability.
- The assessments in this workbook are based on self-reported data. In other words, the accuracy and usefulness of the information is dependent on the information that participants honestly provide about themselves. Assure them that they do not need to share their information with anyone. They can be honest!
- Remind participants that the assessments are exploratory exercises and not a judgment of who they are as human beings.
- The assessments are not a substitute for professional assistance. If you feel any of your participants need more assistance than you can provide, refer them to an appropriate medical professional.

(Continued on the next page)

Format of the *Managing Unwanted Thoughts, Feelings and Actions Workbook* *(Continued)*

Assessment Script

When administering the assessments contained in this workbook, please remember that the assessments can be administered, scored, and interpreted by the client. If working with a group, facilitators should circulate among participants as they complete assessments to ensure that there are no questions. If working with an individual client, facilitators can use the instruction collaboratively.

Please note that instructions to participants, italicized below, are meant to be a guide, so please do not feel you must read or say them word for word.

Tell your participants: *"You will be completing a quick assessment related to the topics we are discussing. Please remember that assessments are powerful tools if you are honest with yourself. Take your time and be truthful in your responses so that your results are an honest reflection of you. Your level of commitment in completing the assessments honestly will determine how much you learn about yourself."*

Allow participants to turn to the first page of their assessment and read the instructions silently to themselves, and then tell them: *"All of the assessments have similar formats, but they have different scales, responses, scoring instructions and methods for interpretation. If you do not understand how to complete the assessment, ask me before you turn the page to begin."*

Then tell them: *"Because there is no time limit for completing the assessments, take your time and work at your own pace. Do not answer the assessments as you think others would like you to answer them or how you think others see you. These assessments are for you to reflect on your life and explore some of the barriers that are keeping you from living a more satisfying life. Before completing each assessment, be sure to read the instructions."*

Make sure that nobody has a question, then tell them, *"Learning about yourself can be a positive and motivating experience. Don't stress about taking the assessments or discovering your results. Just respond honestly and learn as much about yourself as you can."*

Tell participants to turn the page and begin answering with Question 1. Allow sufficient time for all participants to complete their assessment. Answer any questions people have. As people begin to finish, read through the instructions for scoring the assessment. Have participants begin to score their assessment and transfer their scores for interpretation. Make sure that nobody has a question about how to complete the scoring.

Review the purpose of the interpretation table included after each assessment. Tell the participants: *"Remember, this assessment was not designed to label you. Rather, it was designed to develop a baseline of your behaviors. Regardless of how you score on an assessment, consider it a starting point upon which you can develop healthier habits. Take your time, reflect on your results, and note how they compare to what you already know about yourself."*

After participants have completed, scored, and interpreted their assessment, facilitators can use the self-exploration activities included in each module to supplement their traditional tools and techniques to help participants function more effectively.

(Continued on the next page)

Format of the *Managing Unwanted Thoughts, Feelings and Actions Workbook* *(Continued)*

Self-Exploration Activities

This workbook will provide self-exploration activities that can be used to decrease unwanted thoughts, feelings and actions issues. These activities, included after each of the assessments, will prompt self-reflection and promote self-understanding. They use a variety of formats to accommodate all learning styles and foster introspection and promote pro-social behaviors, life skills and coping skills. The activities in each module correlate to the assessments to enable you to identify and select activities quickly and easily.

Self-exploration activities assist participants in self-reflection, enhance self-knowledge, identify potential ineffective behaviors, and teach more effective ways of coping with irrational behaviors. They are is designed to help participants make a series of discoveries that lead to increased social and emotional competencies, as well as to serve as an energizing way to help participants grow personally and professionally. These brief, easy-to-use self-reflection tools are designed to promote insight and self-growth.

Many different types of guided self-exploration activities are provided for you to pick and choose the activities most needed by your participants and the ones that will be most appealing to them. The unique features of the exploration activities make them user-friendly and appropriate for a variety of individual sessions and group sessions.

In some activities, participants will have the opportunity to ...

- explore how they could make changes in their lives to feel better. These activities are designed to help participants reflect on their current life situations, discover new ways of living more effectively, and implement changes in their lives to accommodate these changes.
- journal as a way of enhancing their self-awareness. Through journaling prompts, participants will be able to write about the thoughts, attitudes, feelings, and behaviors that have contributed to, or are currently contributing to, their current life situation. Through journaling, participants are able to safely address their concerns, hopes and dreams for the future.
- investigate their unwanted thoughts, feelings and actions by examining their past for negative patterns and learning new ways of dealing more effectively in the future. These activities are designed to help participants reflect on their lives in ways that will allow them to develop healthier lifestyles.

The Stigma Awareness Approach

It is important that facilitators keep an open mind about mental health issues and the stigma attached to people experiencing these issues. Rather than thinking of people as having a mental disorder, or being mentally ill, the ***Erasing the Stigma of Mental Health Issues through Awareness*** series is designed to help facilitators to diminish the stigma that surrounds people suffering from unwanted thoughts, feelings and actions issues. Stigmas occur when people are unduly labeled, which sets the stage for discrimination and humiliation. Facilitators are able to help to erase the stigma of mental illness through enhanced awareness of the factors that activate the issues, accentuate the depth of the issues, and accelerate awareness and understanding.

To assist you, a section titled ***Erasing the Stigma of Mental Health Issues*** is included to provide activities for helping to erase the stigma associated with unwanted thoughts, feelings and actions issues.

The Awareness Modules

The reproducible awareness modules contained in this workbook will help you identify and select assessments and activities easily and quickly.

Module I: Unwanted Thoughts, Feelings and Actions Symptoms
This module will help participants identify the intensity of their behavioral, cognitive, and affect problems in their lives.

Module II: Life-Management Skills
This module will help participants identify the effectiveness of their present life-management skills.

Module III: Personal Wellness
This module will help participants identify how effective they are in taking care of themselves physically and emotionally.

Module IV: Possibilities
This module will help participants identify the many possibilities available in their lives and careers.

Module V: Erasing the Stigma of Mental Health Issues
This module will help participants explore and refute the stigma of having unwanted thoughts, feelings and actions issues in their lives and the impact that the stigma has on them.

~~~~~~

Our thanks to these professionals who make us look good and who personify people who are dedicated to erasing the stigma of mental health issues.

Art Director – Joy Dey

Assistant Art Director – Mathew Pawlak

Editor and Lifelong Teacher – Eileen Regen

Editorial Director – Carlene Sippola

Proofreader Extraordinaire – Jay Leutenberg

Reviewer – Carol Butler, MS Ed, RN, C

Title-Brainstormer – Kathy Khalsa
~~~~~~

Table of Contents

Module I – Managing Unwanted Thoughts, Feelings and Actions Symptoms Scale 15
Skills Emphasized in Each Activity Handout 16
Thoughts, Feelings and Actions Symptoms Introduction and Directions 17
Thoughts, Feelings and Actions Symptoms Scale 18
Scoring Directions 19
Profile Interpretation 19
Scale Descriptions 19
THOUGHTS: My Unwanted Thinking 20
THOUGHTS: Time to Pay Attention 21
THOUGHTS: My Memory 22
THOUGHTS: Unrealistic Thinking 23
THOUGHTS: My Problems Occur 24
THOUGHTS: The Value of Distractions 25
THOUGHTS: Detective Work 26
FEELINGS: Name Them! 28
FEELINGS: Avoidance 29
FEELINGS: Negative 30
FEELINGS: Positive 31
ACTIONS: My Triggers 32
ACTIONS: A Small Stressful Event 33
ACTIONS: Structuring Your Day 34
ACTIONS: Day-to-Day Tasks 35

Module II – Life-Skills 37
Skills Emphasized in Each Activity Handout 38
Life-Skills Introduction and Directions 39
Life-Skills Scale 40
Scoring Directions 42
Profile Interpretation 42
Scale Descriptions 42
MEDS 43
Potential Support Network 44
Self-Management Skills 45
Life-Skill Skills 46
Managing My Home 48
My Home Management Skills 49
Planning and Organization 50
Stress Reduction 52
Coping Skills for Stress Management 53
My Positive Relationships 56
My Negative Relationships 57
To Disclose or Not? That is the Question! 58
Thoughts, Feelings and/or Actions at Work 59

Table of Contents

Module III – Personal Wellness 61
Skills Emphasized in Each Activity Handout 62
Personal Wellness Introduction and Directions 63
Personal Wellness Scale 64
Scoring Directions 65
Profile Interpretation 65
Scale Descriptions 65
Dine Well? 66
My Favorite Foods! 67
What Do I Eat and Why? 68
My Sleep Routine 71
My Sleep Diary 72
Positive Leisure Time 73
Unable to Relax? 74
Relaxation 75
Reducing Stress 76
Let's Get Physical 77
Problem Solving 78
"To Keep the Body in Good Health …" 81

Module IV – Possibilities 83
Skills Emphasized in Each Activity Handout 84
Possibilities Introduction and Directions 85
Possibilities Scale 86
Scoring Directions 87
Profile Interpretation 87
Scale Descriptions 87
Social Activity Scheduling 88
Social Isolation 89
Breaking the Ice 90
Making Friends 92
Maintaining Friends 93
Everywhere are Signs 94
Possibilities in My Life 96
I Have Dreams 97
Cue Recognition 98
Set Long-Term Goals 99
Set Short-Term Goals 100
My Optimistic Future 101
Work Satisfaction 102
Managing My Unwanted Thoughts, Feelings and Actions at Work 103
My Dream Job 104

Table of Contents

Module V – Erasing the Stigma of Mental Health Issues 107
Erasing the Stigma of Mental Health Issues Introduction............... 109
Skills Emphasized in Each Activity Handout 110
Two Types of Mental Health Stigma.................................. 112
The Stigma of Unwanted Thoughts, Feeling and Actions Issues – THE PAST.. 113
The Stigma of Unwanted Thoughts, Feeling and Actions Issues – THE PRESENT.................................... 114
Are You Ashamed? 115
If We Stamp Out the Stigma 116
Glenn Close said 117
Effects of the Stigma of Unwanted Thoughts, Feeling and Actions Issues 118
The Stigma of Going to a Mental Health Therapist.................... 119
Stereotypes... 120
Coping with the Stigma of Unwanted Thoughts, Feeling and Actions Issues 121
What Can YOU Do?.. 122
My Negative Thoughts 123
Focus on Your Strengths.. 124
Ways I Try to Minimize the Stigma of Unwanted Thoughts, Feeling and Actions Issues 125
Ways I am Treated.. 126
Self-Doubt... 127
A Poster about the STIGMA of People with Unwanted Thoughts, Feeling and Actions Issues.................. 128
A Poster about the ACCEPTANCE of People with Unwanted Thoughts, Feeling and Actions Issues.................. 129
DE-STIGMA-TIZE with the Facts about Mental Health Issues............ 130
Coping with the Stigma of a Mental Health Issue 131
Speak Out Against Stigmas.. 132

MODULE I

Unwanted Thoughts, Feelings and Actions Symptoms

One of the true tests of leadership is the ability to recognize a problem before it becomes an emergency.

~ Arnold H. Glasgow

Name ______________________________

Date ______________

Skills Emphasized in Each Activity Handout

THOUGHTS: My Unwanted Thinking .... page 20
Give examples of unwanted thoughts in nine categories, their frequency and the circumstances in which they occur; identify what is actually happening at those times compared to false beliefs. Identify beliefs that frequently seem real and that suggest the need for therapy and/or medication.

THOUGHTS: Time to Pay Attention .... page 21
Complete seven sentence starters to provide specifics about one's inattentiveness; read and practice twelve attention-related tips.

THOUGHTS: My Memory .... page 22
Describe nine experiences with forgetting and nine ways to remember; read and practice nine memory-related tips.

THOUGHTS: Unrealistic Thinking .... page 23
State four past situations and recognize the accompanying unrealistic thoughts; note current realistic thoughts and identify a recurring theme if applicable.

THOUGHTS: My Problems Occur .... page 24
Depict and describe one's most unwanted thoughts regarding work, family, community and relationships. Select the area that was easiest to describe and state the reasons.

THOUGHTS: The Value of Distractions .... page 25
Document five unwanted thoughts, a distraction for each and ways the distractions help alleviate unwanted thoughts.

THOUGHTS: Detective Work .... page 26
Answer six questions to evaluate whether a recurring thought is reality-based; identify six effects of the evidence.

FEELINGS: Name Them! .... page 28
Name a recent feeling or combinations of feelings, the actions elicited and ways to manage the emotion(s) constructively.

FEELINGS: Avoidance .... page 29
In response to six ways that feelings are avoided, specify what one avoids and the effects; identify the advantages and disadvantages of avoidance.

FEELINGS: Negative .... page 30
Identify when and why one experiences up to twenty-two possible negative emotions.

FEELINGS: Positive .... page 31
Identify when and why one experiences up to twenty-nine positive emotions.

ACTIONS: My Triggers .... page 32
Document five triggers to unwanted actions, recognize the effects and how to manage the effects of each trigger; select the most troublesome trigger and state ways to reduce its impact.

ACTIONS: A Small Stressful Event .... page 33
Answer five insight-oriented questions to explain how a small stressful event led to an unwanted action(s) and what could have been done differently.

ACTIONS: Structuring Your Day .... page 34
Note which issues and actions usually occur mornings, afternoons and/or evenings, why, and what can be done to reduce negative behaviors at these times.

ACTIONS: Day-to-Day Tasks .... page 35
Describe four unwanted action issues, what happens, and how to reduce the behaviors; identify which negative action most affects one's life and what can be done about it.

Unwanted Thoughts, Feelings and Actions Symptoms Scale Introduction and Directions

People who find themselves thinking, feeling and acting in ways they don't really want to, experience certain symptoms that interfere with their life. By being aware of these symptoms, they can learn to manage them.

This assessment contains 30 statements related to your level of unwanted thoughts, feelings and actions' issues. Read each of the statements and decide how much the statement describes you.

- If the statement describes you a lot, circle the number under that column next to that item.
- If the statement describes you sometimes, circle the number under that column next to that item.
- If the statement describes you only a little or not at all, circle the number under that column next to that item

.

In the following example, the circled number under "A Lot" indicates the statement is descriptive of the person completing the inventory a lot of the time.

	A LOT	SOMETIMES	A LITTLE/NONE
I am suspicious of almost everyone	(3)	2	1

This is not a test. Since there are no right or wrong answers, do not spend too much time thinking about your answers. Be sure to respond to every statement.

Turn to the next page and begin.

Unwanted Thoughts, Feelings and Actions Symptoms Scale

	A LOT	SOMETIMES	A LITTLE/NONE
I am suspicious of almost everyone	3	2	1
I hear people who aren't there talking to me	3	2	1
I feel as if I have no control of my actions	3	2	1
I am mistrustful of most people	3	2	1
I cannot focus on my thoughts	3	2	1
I use poor judgment	3	2	1
I find it difficult to process information	3	2	1
My thinking seems disorganized	3	2	1
I am not good at making decisions	3	2	1
I can't remember simple tasks	3	2	1

T - TOTAL = ____________

I have trouble expressing my feelings	3	2	1
I don't seem to have feelings anymore	3	2	1
People say I am cold	3	2	1
I have a difficult time experiencing pleasure	3	2	1
I have swings in my mood	3	2	1
I often show emotions that are different from those I am feeling	3	2	1
I cannot identify my own feelings	3	2	1
I don't know how to react to things that occur	3	2	1
My feelings change for no apparent reason	3	2	1
I feel anxious a lot of the time	3	2	1

F - TOTAL = ____________

I turn people off with my actions	3	2	1
I lack good hygiene	3	2	1
I dress inappropriately	3	2	1
I cannot take care of myself very well	3	2	1
I sleep too much or too little	3	2	1
I engage in inappropriate sexual behavior	3	2	1
I am told I behave strangely	3	2	1
Sometimes I can't get up and move forward	3	2	1
I can't set and work toward goals	3	2	1
I'm involved in dangerous behavior	3	2	1

A - TOTAL = ____________

Unwanted Thoughts, Feelings and Actions Symptoms Scale Scoring Directions

Your thoughts, feelings and actions can interfere with your relationships, work, social activities and, in fact, every aspect of your life. They are probably unwanted by you and/or by the people with whom you interact in your life. This scale is designed to help you understand and identify the symptoms of your unwanted thoughts, feelings and actions.

Add the numbers that you circled. Your total will range from 10 to 30.

Then, transfer this total to the space below:

T	=	Thoughts	TOTAL __________
F	=	Feelings	TOTAL __________
A	=	Actions	TOTAL __________

Profile Interpretation

Individual Score	Result	Indications
10 - 16	Low	Low scores indicate that you are experiencing a low number of symptoms. Complete the following exercises to ensure that you reduce your symptoms even further.
17 - 23	Moderate	Moderate scores indicate that you are experiencing a medium high number of symptoms. Complete the following exercises to ensure that you reduce your symptoms even further.
24 - 30	High	High scores indicate that you are experiencing a very high number of symptoms. Complete the following exercises to that ensure you reduce your symptoms even further.

Scale Descriptions

Thoughts – People scoring High on this scale are experiencing troubled thinking. They may experience negativity, disorganization and confusion, and may find it difficult to process information.

Feelings – People scoring High on this scale have difficulty expressing their emotions. They may show different emotions from what they are actually feeling, and have changes in feelings for no apparent reason.

Actions – People scoring High on this scale are experiencing troubled actions and behaviors. They may behave in strange and dangerous ways, and are challenged with actions and behaviors that they need to take care of themselves.

THOUGHTS: My Unwanted Thinking

Following are some of the most unwanted thoughts that people tend to have. Which ones do you experience? Complete the table that follows. If these thoughts do not occur to you, just write "Does Not Apply."

My Thoughts	How Often I Have These Thoughts	What was Actually Happening?
Example: *Others control what I think*	*My neighbor once told me that I do a bad job of keeping my sidewalk clean and swept. Whenever I go outside, I hear her telling me that even though she's not there.*	*She told me that once and never said it again. I keep dwelling on it.*
Others control what I think		
I believe things that nobody else believes		
I can't trust my thinking		
I don't know what's real and what isn't		
I have magical powers		
Others are plotting against me		
I can't get a hold of my thoughts		
Others are jealous of me		
Other		

Put an asterisk (*) by those thoughts you believe are frequently or always real.
Put a plus (+) by those thoughts that mean you might be in need of therapy and/or medication.

THOUGHTS: Time to Pay Attention

People who experience unwanted thoughts often have difficulty in paying and maintaining attention to their important tasks.

What types of attention problems do you experience?

I lose track of ____

____

I have trouble concentrating ____

____

When I try to do more than one thing at once ____

____

I am most unfocused ____

____

When I get bored I don't think to ____

____

I am unable to learn ____

____

I give up when ____

____

Read and Practice these Attention-Related Tips

- Limit multi-tasking as much as possible.
- Focus on one thing at a time.
- Take frequent breaks.
- Use post-it notes, calendars and/or kitchen timers as reminders.
- Keep things simple and as direct as possible.
- Try deep breathing when you start drifting away.
- Avoid distractions.
- Walk outside for a few moments of fresh air when bored.
- Use self-talk. *(I can do this!)*
- On the computer? One window at a time.
- Put cell phone in another room.
- Step back and think, *Was this thought realistic?*

THOUGHTS: My Memory

People who have experienced issues with their thought-processes, often have a difficult time remembering. These memory problems can greatly affect day-to-day functioning.

In the spaces that follow, describe the types of tasks you have trouble remembering.

What I Forget	Describe an Experience	How Can I Remember?
Example: *I forget scheduled appointments*	*I forgot a very important doctor's appointment. I was charged for the appointment and had to wait two more weeks.*	*I can put a post-it note on the refrigerator.*
I forget scheduled appointments		
I forget to take my medications		
I can't remember where I put things		
I lose track of money		
I forget names		
I can't remember what I read		
I forget important dates		
I can't remember directions		
Other		

Read and Practice these Memory-Related Tips

- Date book
- Timer
- Postie notes
- Make lists
- Calendar in: phone, pad, computer, house, pocket
- Pay attention
- Put things always in the same place
- Always carry a notebook
- Write everything in the notebook
- Don't lose the notebook!

THOUGHTS: Unrealistic Thinking

Many people have a hard time understanding what is real and what is not. This thinking can get in the way of reality and interfere with daily functioning. There are times when you will need to perform a reality check to make sure that what you are experiencing is real.

It is important to replace unrealistic thinking with realistic thinking.

Name a Past Situation	My Unrealistic Thoughts at the Time	My Realistic Thoughts Now
Example: I was sick and home all alone.	*My partner isn't here and doesn't even care.*	*Even though I was all alone, before going to work he asked if it was okay and then called several times during the day to check on me.*

Is there a recurring theme related to your unrealistic thinking? **Describe it.** ______________________

____

____

____

THOUGHTS: My Problems Occur ...

One of the first tasks you need to complete, in order to manage your unrealistic thinking issues, is to determine where these thoughts occur the most.

In the spaces below, describe through writing, doodling or drawing the situations in which your thinking issues occur most often, in these four areas of your life.

In my work and/or volunteer life	In my home and/or family life
In my community	In my relationships

Which area of your life was the easiest to describe, and why? ____________________

____

____

____

THOUGHTS: The Value of Distractions

Distracting yourself from an unwanted thought may help you take your mind off of it for a while.

What are some of the ways you can distract yourself when you are experiencing thoughts you don't want to have?

My Unwanted Thoughts	How I Can Distract Myself	How This Helps Me
Example: I am so sad about my loss	*I can go to a movie.*	*I get absorbed in the movie and forget about my own issues for a couple of hours. I feel better and readier to cope afterwards.*

THOUGHTS: Detective Work

You need a specific process for challenging your unrealistic thinking. The process of challenging and changing our automatic, and often unrealistic thoughts, begin by taking a good hard look at them. To find out whether or not your thoughts are true, you need to gather and examine specific evidence.

You are about to be a detective. Pick one situation.

____

____

____

Find the facts and gather the evidence related to your thinking.

Here are some helpful questions to ask yourself:

- Where is the evidence (or proof) that my thoughts and beliefs are true?
- Is there any evidence that disproves my thoughts and/or beliefs?
- How can I be positive that my thoughts and/or beliefs are true?
- Are there facts that I'm ignoring or that I've overlooked?
- What other explanations could there possibly be?
- How realistic are my thoughts and beliefs?

Detective Work is looking for evidence that does or does not support your thoughts and beliefs. You are asking questions to find evidence to challenge. This provides insight allowing you to consider whether or not your thoughts are true.

After you have asked the above questions, the following questions will help you evaluate how the realistic (or unrealistic) nature of your thinking affects you:

- Are there other ways of viewing the situation?
- How might someone else view the situation?
- If that person's view is different than mine, how do I evaluate that?
- How important is it for me to keep thinking my own way?
- Am I open to someone else's thoughts about the situation?
- How do I decide whether to listen to what the other person has to say?

(Continued on the next page)

THOUGHTS: Detective Work *(Continued)*

Now You Try. Below think about your most prevalent, recurring thought that may or may not be realistic.

Focus on one thought, ____

____

____

Now evaluate it by answering the following questions:

- Where is the evidence (or proof) that my thought is true? ____________________

  ____
- What evidence disproves my thought? ____________________

  ____
- How can I be positive that my thought is true?____________________

  ____
- What are the facts that I'm ignoring or that I've overlooked? ____________________

  ____
- What other explanations could there possibly be? ____________________

  ____
- How realistic are my thoughts?____________________

  ____

Now write about how it is affecting you. Answer the questions that follow:

- How does the evidence (or proof) that my thought is true affect me? ____________________

  ____
- How does the evidence that disproves my thought affect me? ____________________

  ____
- How does being positive that my thought is true affect me?____________________

  ____
- How do the facts that I'm ignoring or that I've overlooked affect me? ____________________

  ____
- How do other possible explanations affect me? ____________________

  ____
- How does a realistic thought affect me? ____________________

  ____

FEELINGS: Name Them!

For people who experience emotional issues, an important strategy is to name the emotions you feel. Try the exercise that follows. Focus on one frequent feeling.

---

1. Start to observe your feeling, but don't become overwhelmed.
2. Name a feeling and describe whether it is a pure feeling or some combination of feelings. For example, a person could feel a combination of jealousy, love and anger.
3. Don't resist the feeling, amplify, analyze, or judge yourself for having it.
4. Think about the actions that this feeling brings on.
5. Think about ways to manage the feeling constructively.

Remember that feelings come and go, and that you do have them. It is important that you experience them and learn effective ways to manage them. Fill in the lines below recalling a recent negative feeling. Now you try.

1. Start to observe one of your feelings, but don't become overwhelmed. What are you feeling?

   ____

   ____

   ____

2. Describe whether it is a pure feeling or a combination of feelings.

   ____

   ____

   ____

3. Don't resist the feeling, or amplify it, or analyze it, or judge yourself for having it. Just observe it. How does this feel? Explain.

   ____

   ____

   ____

4. Think about the actions this feeling brings on. What does the feeling urge you to do?

   ____

   ____

   ____

5. Think about ways to manage the feeling constructively. How can you manage the feeling effectively?

   ____

   ____

   ____

FEELINGS: Avoidance

When you avoid your feelings, it often leads to different types of difficulties.
People avoid their feelings for a variety of reasons.
Think about how you avoid your feelings, what you avoid and the effects it has on you.

Ways I Avoid My Feelings	What I Avoid	The Effect This Has on Me
Example: I stay away from places that might trigger feelings.	*I don't go to the café I used to go to before we broke up.*	*I feel sad every time I go by because it brings back bittersweet memories, but I miss out because it's very convenient and the food is great!*
I stay away from places that might trigger feelings.		
I stay away from people who might trigger feelings.		
I try not to think about sad memories.		
I try not to focus on my sad feelings.		
I try to replace one feeling with another feeling.		
Other		

What do you feel is the **advantage** of avoiding your feelings? Give an example. ________________

____

What do you feel is the **disadvantage** of avoiding your feelings? Give an example.________________

____

FEELINGS: Negative

Many people regularly experience a variety of unhealthy, negative feelings. You can benefit from identifying the types of feelings that you experience most often.

On the list below check the negative feelings that you experience most often. Next to the feeling, write when and why.

- ☐ Alienated ______________________________
- ☐ Angry ______________________________
- ☐ Annoyed ______________________________
- ☐ Anxious ______________________________
- ☐ Confused ______________________________
- ☐ Depressed ______________________________
- ☐ Discouraged ______________________________
- ☐ Embarrassed ______________________________
- ☐ Empty ______________________________
- ☐ Frustrated ______________________________
- ☐ Isolated ______________________________
- ☐ Mistrustful ______________________________
- ☐ Misunderstood ______________________________
- ☐ Persecuted ______________________________
- ☐ Scared ______________________________
- ☐ Tired ______________________________
- ☐ Unsafe ______________________________
- ☐ Other ______________________________
- ☐ Other ______________________________
- ☐ Other ______________________________
- ☐ Other ______________________________
- ☐ Other ______________________________

FEELINGS: Positive

People with emotional issues experience a variety of unhealthy, negative feelings but also experience healthy, positive feelings – often at the same time. You can benefit from identifying the types of positive emotions that you experience most often. It is common to have some negative feelings, even when you are in the midst of positive feelings and situations.

On the list below check the positive feelings that you experience most often. Next to each feeling write when and why.

- ☐ Accepted ______________________________
- ☐ Calm ______________________________
- ☐ Cautious ______________________________
- ☐ Confident ______________________________
- ☐ Creative ______________________________
- ☐ Curious ______________________________
- ☐ Determined ______________________________
- ☐ Ecstatic ______________________________
- ☐ Excited ______________________________
- ☐ Fulfilled ______________________________
- ☐ Grateful ______________________________
- ☐ Happy ______________________________
- ☐ Interested ______________________________
- ☐ Involved ______________________________
- ☐ Loved ______________________________
- ☐ Lovestruck ______________________________
- ☐ Optimistic ______________________________
- ☐ Peaceful ______________________________
- ☐ Pleasantly surprised ______________________________
- ☐ Proud ______________________________
- ☐ Relieved ______________________________
- ☐ Safe ______________________________
- ☐ Thoughtful ______________________________
- ☐ Trustful ______________________________
- ☐ Understood ______________________________
- ☐ Vulnerable ______________________________
- ☐ Other ______________________________
- ☐ Other ______________________________

ACTIONS: My Triggers

It is important to explore the triggers of your unwanted actions. These triggers can come from any area of your life including work, community or your relationships.

In the table that follows, the triggers of your actions.

What Trigger Sets Me Off	How it Affects Me	How I Can Manage the Stress of this Trigger
Example: When I don't have the money to pay a bill.	*I'm up most of the night worrying. I'm grouchy at home and work. Then I think about doing something illegal to get more money.*	*I need to get a second job, develop a budget, discuss the situation openly with my family and talk about careful spending.*

My most troublesome trigger is ____

____

To reduce the impact of this trigger, I can ____________________________________

____

____

____

ACTIONS: A Small Stressful Event

Small stressful events (being asked to do something you don't like to do at work, kids yelling, technology won't work, etc.) can trigger actions-of-the-moment in which you feel badly and regret later.

Think back to the last time you experienced a personal action and behavior issue.

What was happening at the time?

____

____

____

Who were you with?

____

____

____

Why did you get so upset?

____

____

____

What did you do?

____

____

____

What could you have done differently that might have had a more positive outcome?

____

____

____

ACTIONS: Structuring your Day

Eliminating surprises in your environment and maintaining a structured daily routine can help to make day-to-day tasks more manageable, and decrease the chances for behavior issues. Breaking up the day with tasks can greatly improve your chances. **Describe your daily routine**.

Time of the Day	What I Do	Why Does this Matter?	What Can I Do About It?
Example: Morning	*I am tired, unpleasant, and not sociable the first hour after I wake up in the morning.*	*My family avoids me and hates when they need to ask me a question.*	*Get to bed an hour earlier. Get up an hour earlier. Read the paper, have a hot beverage and/or exercise. Greet my family with a smile!*
Morning			
Afternoon			
Evening			

During which parts of the day are you most apt to experience an action you will regret later?

____

Why do you think you experience these actions during this time of the day? ____________________

____

What can you do to reduce these behavior issues during this part of your day? ________________

____

____

ACTIONS: Day-to-Day Tasks

Unwanted actions can interfere with your ability to carry out tasks. Think about how they are affecting your home life and career.

In the spaces below, describe your unwanted actions.

My Unwanted Action Issues	What Happens?	How I Can Reduce These Behaviors
Example: When I am asked to mow the lawn I make up excuses, and when I'm reminded I yell and accuse people of nagging me.	*The lawn doesn't get cut, my family is angry at me because of my yelling, and I am embarrassed that it looks so awful. I eventually end up doing it - too late.*	*Make a commitment. A date and time when I will do it each and every week without anyone telling me to do it. And I'll commit to being pleasant when doing it.*

Which action is negatively affecting your life the most? ______________________

____

____

What can you do about it? ______________________

____

____

MODULE II

Life Skills

Don't wait until everything is just right. It will never be perfect. There will always be challenges, obstacles and less than perfect conditions. So what. Get started now. With each step you take, you will grow stronger and stronger, more and more skilled, more and more self-confident and more and more successful.

~ Mark Victor Hansen

Name ____

Date __________________________

Skills Emphasized in Each Activity Handout

MEDS .... page 43
Prepare a list of meds to take to physician; document meds' benefits, ways to reduce side effects, compliance issues, and possible changes to discuss.

Potential Support Network .... page 44
Name five potential supportive persons and state what to share about oneself and how these people can help.

Self-Management Skills .... page 45
State ways one manages self and actions to improve regarding: meds, finances, household, relaxation, nutrition, grooming, work and other categories.

Life-Skill Skills .... page 46
Rate oneself on ten point continuums and explain each score regarding: bathing, grooming, house cleaning, working; managing stress, moods and meds; developing and maintaining friendships and relationships; driving effectively, keeping appointments and other categories.

Managing My Home .... page 48
Document four household chores that one does and when; identify four chores that one cannot currently do, and note who or what can help.

My Home Management Skills .... page 49
Complete six sentence starters describing task management at home and in the community, e.g., shopping and driving.

Planning and Organizing .... page 50
Structure a daily schedule noting ways to simplify tasks; document a weekly to-do list and prioritize.

Stress Reduction .... page 52
Read more than twelve suggested physical or recreational activities; for each document the amount of time spent per week, how one feels when engaging in the activity and/or reasons for non-involvement.

Coping Skills for Stress Management .... page 53
Practice deep breathing and meditation, share the humor in a situation, identify ways to avoid and/or handle stressful situations, list ways to find a support group and to pamper oneself; brainstorm key words for an Internet search regarding relaxation techniques; research, document and describe to peers three stress management skills.

My Positive Relationships .... page 56
Identify six relationships noting how one's thoughts, feelings and actions issues have affected and strengthened these relationships. State which relationship one is most pleased about and why.

My Negative Relationships .... page 57
Name five relationships and describe how one's issues have affected and weakened these relationships; note which relationship one is saddest about and ways to repair it.

To Disclose or Not? That is the Question! .... page 58
Read six risks and six benefits of disclosing unwanted thoughts, feelings and actions issues in the workplace; declare one's choice to disclose or not, and the reasons.

Thoughts, Feelings and/or Actions at Work .... page 59
Identify how one's unwanted thoughts, feelings and/or actions affect five or more relationships at work and how to reduce the effects.

Life-Skills Scale
Introduction and Directions

Learning life skills to manage the effects of unwanted feelings issues is important. Consider ways to develop important life skills in five major aspects of your life:

I. Self-Management
II. Home Management
III. Daily Chores Management
IV. Relationship Management
V. Career Management

This assessment contains 30 statements designed to help you explore how your thoughts, feelings and actions may be affecting how you manage your life. Read each of the statements and decide whether the statement describes you or not. If the statement does describe you, circle the number in the TRUE column next to that item. If the statement does not describe you, circle the number in the FALSE column next to that item.

In the following example, the circled 1 indicates the statement does not describe the person completing the inventory:

When it comes to managing myself…	**TRUE**	**FALSE**
I take my medication when I need to	2	(1)

This is not a test. Since there are no right or wrong answers, do not spend too much time thinking about your answers. Be sure to respond to every statement.

Turn to the next page and begin.

Life-Skills Scale

When it comes to managing myself...	TRUE	FALSE
I take my medication when I need to	2	1
I can manage my money without assistance	2	1
I cannot dress myself without help	1	2
I cannot prepare my food and/or eat by myself	1	2
I can perform basic bathing and grooming functions	2	1
I can leave my house by myself	2	1

I TOTAL = ____________

When it comes to managing my home...	TRUE	FALSE
I am not very neat or clean	1	2
I participate in household maintenance tasks	2	1
I have trouble shopping for groceries and necessities	1	2
I am able to do my laundry	2	1
I cannot clean my house	1	2
I respect my property and the property of others	2	1

II TOTAL = ____________

When it comes to managing my daily chores...	TRUE	FALSE
I manage my time well	1	2
I know when and how to relax	2	1
I am not good at planning	1	2
I don't have much clutter in my house	2	1
I have too many obligations to finish everything	1	2
I don't do what I need to because of too many responsibilities	1	2

III TOTAL = ____________

(Continued on the next page)

Life-Skills Scale *(Continued)*

When it comes to managing my relationships…	TRUE	FALSE
I have good social skills	2	1
I no longer get together with my friends	1	2
I act appropriately and politely in social situations	2	1
I am friendly with people I don't know	2	1
I withdraw from friends and family members	1	2
I find it difficult to talk with others	1	2

IV TOTAL = ____________________

When it comes to managing my career…	TRUE	FALSE
I perform well at work	2	1
I don't trust people at work	1	2
It's hard for me to concentrate on the job	1	2
I can't keep a job	1	2
I get confused easily at work	1	2
I have good job-related skills	2	1

V TOTAL = ____________________

Life-Skills Scale Scoring Directions

The Life Skills Scale you just completed is designed to measure the effects of your thoughts, feelings and actions and your ability to manage everyday life. For each of the sections on the previous pages, count the scores you circled. Put that total on the line marked TOTAL at the end of each section.

Then, transfer your total to the space below:

I	=	Self-Management	TOTAL ___________
II	=	Home Management	TOTAL ___________
III	=	Daily Chores Management	TOTAL ___________
IV	=	Relationship Management	TOTAL ___________
V	=	Career Management	TOTAL ___________

Add your five scores together for your Grand TOTAL ___________

Profile Interpretation

Individual Score	Grand Total	Result	Indications
6 - 7	30 - 39	Low	Low scores indicate that you are affected too much by your lack of life skills. Complete the following exercises to improve these skills.
8 -10	40 - 49	Moderate	Moderate scores indicate that you are being somewhat affected by lack of life skills. Complete the following exercises to reduce the effects.
11 - 12	50 - 60	High	High scores indicate that you have excellent life skills. Complete the following exercises to continue polishing your life skills.

Scale Descriptions

I. Self-Management – People scoring High on this scale are able to manage life skills such as medications, finances, eating well, maintaining basic grooming functions and taking care of themselves.

II. Home Management – People scoring High on this scale are able to manage life skills such as household maintenance, cleaning, shopping, and taking care of their property.

III. Daily Chores Management – People scoring High on this scale are able to manage life skills such as stress from daily chores. They are able to plan, organize and balance relaxation with responsibilities.

IV. Relationship Management – People scoring High on this scale are able to manage relationship skills. They have effective social skills, act appropriate, and can easily interact with other people.

V. Career Management – People scoring High on this scale manage life skills such as having a job and performing well. They do not have difficulty completing assigned tasks or interacting with their supervisors and co-workers.

GRAND TOTAL – High scores on all five scales indicate that the person is functioning well with their total life skills management. The following pages will be helpful to all participants, no matter how they scored.

MEDS

If you are taking medications, it is important to take them regularly and as directed by a physician. A problem for people with thoughts, feelings and actions issues occur when they either forget to take their meds regularly or stop taking them altogether. Without your meds, it might be very difficult to manage your life. People with thoughts, feelings and actions issues often need to take medication in order to make positive changes in their lives.

Medications can be extremely helpful, but they may also have unwanted side effects which can deter people from taking them. It is important to talk to physicians, research ways to deal with side-affects, and learn which reactions to report immediately.

In the table below, identify all of the medications you have taken and are currently taking; note how regularly you take them; list the side effects; explain how you can minimize those side effects; and describe how the meds help you. Include medications prescribed by a physician as well as over-the-counter medicines.

My Medications	Take Regularly?	Side Effects	How I Can Minimize the Side-Effects	How the Meds Help Me

If you have stopped taking a medication, why? ______________________________

____

____

Have you spoken to your physician about this? If not, why not? ______________________________

____

What medication changes or additions do you need to speak about with your physician?

____

____

Take this completed paper with you to your medical professional on your next visit.

Potential Support Network

Educating (learning and talking about one's issues) and asking for support from one's partner, family members and trusted friends and adults about thoughts, feelings and actions can be unbelievably helpful. In addition, one can involve these important people in treatment when possible. They can help spot symptoms, track actions and behaviors, gain perspective, remind you to take meds, accompany you to appointments, provide encouraging feedback, and help you to make a plan to cope with any future crises.

Who are the family members, trusted friends and adults with whom you feel safe in confiding and who can support you? In the table below, identify those people and how they can support you. Some people support in one way (example, listening) and others can support in other ways (example, encouraging). Think about each person and how you can benefit from that person's particular strengths.

Potential Supportive Person	How and What Will I Tell This Person About Me and My Needs	How This Person Can Support Me

Which one of the people above will you contact first? ______________________

When? ______________________

____

____

Self-Management Skills

Your ability to manage the daily tasks required to live effectively is very important for all people. Because you may be experiencing unwanted thoughts, feelings and actions, learning self-management skills may be more difficult. The purpose of this assessment is to discover those aspects you are managing well and those you may not be managing well.

In the table below, journal about how effectively you feel you are managing each aspect of yourself.

Self-Management Areas	How I am Managing It	What I Could do Better	Actions I Will Take to Improve
Example: Medications	*I can't remember if I have taken them or not.*	*Find a better system for knowing when to take them.*	*I will purchase a weekly pillbox to help me remember.*
Medications			
Finances			
Household			
Relaxation			
Eating			
Grooming			
Work			
Other			
Other			

Life-Skill Skills

People with thoughts, feelings and actions issues often find it difficult to perform ordinary life skills. By becoming more aware of deficiencies in your life skills, you can develop a plan to overcome them.

For each of the following items in the next two pages, place an X over the spot on the line that you think describes your level of life-skills.

	Gloomy	Sunny

Personal Grooming 0------------------------------5------------------------------10

Explain ____

____

Work 0------------------------------5------------------------------10

Explain ____

____

Deal with stressful experiences 0------------------------------5------------------------------10

Explain ____

____

Manage my moods 0------------------------------5------------------------------10

Explain ____

____

Develop friendships 0------------------------------5------------------------------10

Explain ____

____

Maintain friendships 0------------------------------5------------------------------10

Explain ____

____

(Continued on the next page)

Life-Skill Skills *(Continued)*

	Gloomy	Sunny
Clean my house	**0-----------------------------5-----------------------------10**	

Explain ____

____

Bathe **0-----------------------------5-----------------------------10**

Explain ____

____

Drive effectively **0-----------------------------5-----------------------------10**

Explain ____

____

Keep appointments **0-----------------------------5-----------------------------10**

Explain ____

____

Manage my medications **0-----------------------------5-----------------------------10**

Explain ____

____

Maintain my relationships **0-----------------------------5-----------------------------10**

Explain ____

____

Other **0-----------------------------5-----------------------------10**

Explain ____

____

Other **0-----------------------------5-----------------------------10**

Explain ____

____

Managing My Home

People who have thoughts, feelings and actions issues tend to have difficulty in managing their household.

Identify both the ways you are able to manage your home and the chores you need help in managing.

Important Chores in My Household	Things I DO	When I Do Them
Example: *Maintaining the tile floor.*	*Clean it.*	*Mop it on Wednesday and Saturday.*

Important Chores in My Household	Things I CANNOT Do	Who or What Can Help Me
Example: *Shop for Groceries.*	*Drive to the store.*	*I can catch the bus that stops up the road.*

My Home Management Skills

Maintaining a home can be a difficult, yet critical, task for people with unwanted thoughts, feelings and actions issues.

For each of these sentence starters, write how you are managing tasks in your home. If any do not apply to you, write "not my issue" and explain why.

Example: I shop for groceries every Saturday.

I shop ____

____

____

I cook____

____

____

I drive ____

____

____

I clean ____

____

____

I take care of ____

____

____

I do ____

____

____

Planning and Organizing

The ability to plan and organize your life is an important life skill, and yet it can be one of the most difficult life skills to implement on a daily basis.

The following is designed to help you add more structure to your life.

My Schedule

- Develop a schedule to help you become more organized.
- What activities do you do the same time every day?

Simplify Tasks

- Break tasks down into steps. If you need to clean your house, break the task down. Work on one room each day until finished.
- What important tasks in your daily routine can you break down into smaller tasks to be more manageable?

(Continued on the next page)

Planning and Organizing *(continued)*

Making lists of things you need to do and then crossing the items off the list after they are completed is one of the most effective ways of being organized.

List the important things you need to do each week. Try it below:

My *To-Do List*

1) ____________________

2) ____________________

3) ____________________

4) ____________________

5) ____________________

6) ____________________

7) ____________________

8) ____________________

Prioritize

Now take your list and prioritize it by putting the most important things you need to do first, and then less important tasks after those. Try it below:

1) ____________________

2) ____________________

3) ____________________

4) ____________________

5) ____________________

6) ____________________

7) ____________________

8) ____________________

Stress REDUCTION

Stress is a major trigger for people who experience thoughts, feelings and actions issues. You can do many things to reduce stress in your life.

Think about the amount of time you participate in physical activities each week, how you feel, and if you don't participate, why not.

Physical Activity	How Much Time Per Week?	How It Makes Me Feel When I Do It	I Don't Do It Because …
Example: Dance	*A half an hour a day. 3-1/2 hours a week.*	*I put on music and dance alone. I feel free.*	
Dance			
Exercise			
Listen to music			
Walk, jog and/or walk a pet			
Spend time outdoors			
Ride a bicycle			
Engage in aerobic activities			
Enjoy a picnic			
Practice yoga, tai chi, etc.			
Volunteer			
Meditate			
Read			
Use social media			
Other			

Return to the list and put a check by the activities you are willing to increase regularly.

Coping Skills for Stress Management

Below, and on the next page, are some coping skills for dealing with stress, especially the stress from daily hassles. Consider a variety of techniques that may help you relax.

Deep Breathing – Deep breathing involves inhaling slowly through your nose (you should notice your abdomen going up and down) and exhaling through your mouth. Repeat this process by continuing to take long, slow deep breaths that raise and lower your abdomen. Continue this process for at least five to ten minutes or until your mood has lightened. Now you try it. Then describe below how you felt during the deep breathing exercise.

____

____

____

____

Avoid Stressful Situations –Sometimes you can avoid situations that are likely to cause stress. You know what they are. If you are uneasy in crowds, do what you can to avoid these situations. List your stress-producing situations and what you can do to avoid them.

____

____

____

____

Handling Stressful Situations – Sometimes you need to face situations that are likely to cause you stress. If you must be in a crowd, take a support person with you or make a time-out plan. List your stress-producing situations and ways you can handle them.

____

____

____

____

Meditation – Meditation can help you to focus your attention on one thing at a time. For example, you could take a few minutes and gaze at an object of your choice (a candle, cup, flower, etc.) at your eye level. Gaze at the object for a few minutes. Note its size, shape and color. If you become distracted, simply return your gaze to the object. You could also count your breaths by counting one for each time you inhale and two when you exhale. Continue counting your breaths until you reach ten, and then begin again with one. Try it and describe below what happened to you - the thoughts running through your head - and your mood.

____

____

____

____

(Continued on the next page)

Coping Skills for Stress Management *(Continued)*

Find a Support Group – Support groups are important for sharing your experiences with people in a similar situation. How can you find a support group in your community? If there isn't one available, how can you start one?

____

____

____

____

Engage in relaxing and fun activities – If you have enjoyed hobbies in the past, now should be no different. Think about the hobbies you had at one time, but gave up because of your thoughts, feelings and action issues. List those hobbies, why you stopped, and how you will begin engaging in them again.

____

____

____

____

Laugh More – It is essential to try to see the funny side or opposite side of every situation. What types of situation could you flip around so that even if it wasn't funny when it happened, it will seem funny now?

____

____

____

____

Make Time for Yourself – Start scheduling time each day to pamper yourself. You could schedule a massage, good book, long bath, movie, etc. How can you pamper yourself?

____

____

____

____

There are many more relaxation techniques may be found on reliable Internet sources.

(Continued on the next page)

Coping Skills for Stress Management *(Continued)*

Reliable Internet Resources for Relaxation Techniques

Brainstorm with others in the room the key words you can put into the internet to find different relaxation techniques.

List them:

________	________	________
________	________	________
________	________	________
________	________	________
________	________	________
________	________	________

Search the Internet and find three relaxation techniques that appeal to you. Check the details for each and write a brief description about them.

1. ______________________________

____

____

2. ______________________________

____

____

3. ______________________________

____

____

Everyone can share the information that they have learned with each other.

My Positive Relationships

Coping with unwanted thoughts, feelings and actions issues can affect your personal relationships in a positive way with the support of the positive people in your life.

In the table below, describe the relationships that these issues have made stronger.

My Relationships	The Effect My Issues Had on This Relationship	How the Relationship Is Stronger
Example: My uncle	*I didn't know who to turn to. He had similar issues in the past. I turned to him.*	*We see each other more often now. He helps me by listening and even advising me. He is helped by feeling good that he uses his experiences to help me.*

Which relationship are you most pleased about and why?

(Example: I love my uncle and value our new found relationship.)

My Negative Relationships

Coping with unwanted thoughts, feelings and actions can affect your personal relationships in a negative way.

In the table below, describe the relationships that these issues have made weaker.

My Relationships	The Effect My Issues Had on This Relationship	How the Relationship Deteriorated
Sister	*I can't talk to her because she is very judgmental and she would judge me.*	*We drifted further apart when she saw I had problems and didn't talk to her about them.*

Which relationship are you most sad about and how can you repair it?

(Example: Tell my sister I want to tell her something and I'll ask her to promise not to judge me).

____

____

____

To Disclose or Not? That is the Question!

The decision to disclose an unwanted thought, feeling and/or action issue in the workplace is a difficult one. Some of the risks and benefits:

RISKS

- Stigmas remain strong in the workplace
- You may be treated differently
- It may be more difficult to advance in your career
- Your supervisor may think you cannot handle stressful situations
- Your co-workers may treat you differently
- You may be judged by others

BENEFITS

- You will no longer have to hide the fact of your issue
- You can ask for accommodations to be made
- Your co-workers can learn more about your unwanted thoughts, feelings and/or actions issues
- You can relax a bit
- You might be able to build a strong support network
- You might be able to find a mentor who can help you adjust

Now that you see the risks and benefits of disclosing your unwanted thought, feelings and/or action issues, describe which you will choose to do and why?

Thoughts, Feelings and/or Actions Issues at Work

Your unwanted thoughts, feelings and/or actions issues may be affecting your performance at work, your ability to move up in an organization, and ultimately your career development.

In the table below, identify all of the ways your issues are affecting your performance on your job.

A Person I Work with	How My Issues Affect This Person	Affect This Person Less
Example: *A Co-Worker* *Sam*	*He doesn't seem to like working with me because I am inconsistent and he feels he can't count on me.*	*Explain to him that I am having some issues, I know I'm inconsistent, but I am working on it. I can ask him to be patient and assure him I'll try harder. I can ask him to suggest ways I can become more consistent.*
A Co-Worker ____________		
A Co-Worker ____________		
A Co-Worker ____________		
A Co-Worker ____________		
A Co-Worker ____________		
A Co-Worker ____________		
A Co-Worker ____________		

MODULE III

Personal Wellness

Wellness is the complete integration of body, mind, and spirit - the realization that everything we do, think, feel, and believe has an effect on our state of well-being.

~ Greg Anderson

Name ______________________________

Date ______________________

Skills Emphasized in Each Activity Handout

Foods I Currently Eat .... page 66
Document foods and liquids consumed each day last week and identify healthier substitutions.

Dine Well? .... page 67
Read a Virginia Woolf quotation, describe what she might think of one's food choices; provide personal definitions of "thinking well, sleeping well, dining well."

My Favorite Foods! .... page 68
Draw one's four favorite foods and describe why they are healthy or not; state ways to promise oneself to make better choices!

What Do I Consume and Why? .... page 69
Identify food, fluids and substances one consumes from among twelve categories; distinguish which are taken in adequate amounts, which to increase and decrease.

My Sleep Routine .... page 71
Document one's sleep routine compared to six suggestions; identify what needs to change to promote more restful sleep.

My Sleep Diary .... page 72
Record quantity and quality of sleep on a weekly sleep diary page; pinpoint possible differences in thoughts, feelings and actions related to restful and wakeful sleep.

Positive Leisure Time .... page 73
Describe leisure activities, how they help and why one doesn't do more, in these and other categories: creative, educational, social, solitary, spiritual, physical, family/community; share related discoveries.

Unable to Relax? .... page 74
Read five and identify two additional reasons why one may be unable to relax; for each reason identify the detrimental effects and what can be done to promote relaxation.

Relaxation .... page 75
Review six calming activity suggestions and add one's own; for each activity identify its benefits and ways to increase its frequency.

Reducing Stress .... page 76
Read descriptions of six stress management techniques and add other(s); note which have or have not been tried, whether they are liked or disliked and why.

Let's Get Physical .... page 77
Document amounts of time devoted to more than twelve suggested physical activities, the benefits of each and reasons for not engaging in specific ones; choose and/or add activities to do more often.

Problem Solving I, II and III .... page 78
Practice problem solving steps: explain its aspects, possible solutions, difficulties, requirements and resources; identify the best solution and break it down into manageable steps. Implement the solution and then state whether it was effective; identify a different solution if necessary. Identify an anticipated future stressful situation, list the steps to prepare to problem solve, including what one will say and what one will do.

"To Keep the Body in Good Health …" .... page 81
Explain why one agrees or disagrees with a Buddha quotation about the link between body and mind; describe current efforts and what more one can do to promote physical and mental health.

Personal Wellness Scale Introduction and Directions

Personal wellness is essential in maintaining good mental health. Good choices related to your life style include having a healthy food plan, sleeping well, relaxing, exercising, and being able to solve problems effectively. These choices can significantly enhance your ability to live well.

This assessment is designed to help you explore how healthy your lifestyle choices have been. This assessment contains 25 statements related to your level of personal wellness. Read each of the statements and decide how completely the statement describes you.

- If the statement describes you a lot, circle the number under that column next to that item.
- If the statement describes you sometimes, circle the number under that column next to that item.
- If the statement describes you only a little or not at all, circle the number under that column next to that item.

In the following example, the circled number under "A Lot" indicates the statement is descriptive of the person completing the inventory a lot of the time.

	A LOT	SOMETIMES	A LITTLE/NONE
I eat a healthy, balanced diet	(3)	2	1

This is not a test. Since there are no right or wrong answers, do not spend too much time thinking about your answers. Be sure to respond to every statement.

Turn to the next page and begin.

Personal Wellness Scale

	A LOT	SOMETIMES	A LITTLE/NONE
I eat a healthy, balanced diet	3	2	1
I eat regularly and I avoid changes in my blood sugar	3	2	1
I keep my home stocked with healthy foods	3	2	1
I eat healthy snacks like fruits and vegetables	3	2	1
I avoid too many fats	3	2	1

FP - TOTAL = ______________

I stick to a regular routine before going to bed	3	2	1
I avoid caffeine after dinner	3	2	1
I avoid alcohol and nicotine before bed	3	2	1
I try to relax before going to bed	3	2	1
I avoid napping so I can sleep well at night	3	2	1

S - TOTAL = ______________

I am able to relax	3	2	1
I like to take walks	3	2	1
I build some relaxation into my daily routine	3	2	1
When stressed, I remember to breathe deeply and slowly	3	2	1
I think about happy memories to help me relax	3	2	1

R - TOTAL = ______________

I exercise to stay healthy	3	2	1
I play sports	3	2	1
I engage in physical activity by working in the yard	3	2	1
I do aerobic exercises	3	2	1
I do yoga/flexibility training	3	2	1

E - TOTAL = ______________

I understand why I become upset or stressed	3	2	1
I have a method for solving problems	3	2	1
I brainstorm realistic solutions to my problems	3	2	1
I ask others for their opinions before solving problems	3	2	1
I am able to choose the best solutions to my problems	3	2	1

SP - TOTAL = ______________

Personal Wellness Scale
Scoring Directions

Personal wellness is an overlooked aspect that is critical in your ability to overcome stress related to experiencing unwanted thoughts, feelings and actions issues.

The Personal Wellness Scale is designed to help you explore your level of personal wellness. For the scale you just completed, add the numbers that you circled. This score will give you some sense of the strength of your personal wellness. Your total will range from 25 to 75.

Then, transfer your total to the space below:

FP = Food Plan TOTAL __________

S = Sleep TOTAL __________

R = Relaxation TOTAL __________

E = Exercise TOTAL __________

SP = Solving Problems TOTAL __________

Level of Personal Wellness Grand TOTAL __________

Profile Interpretation

Individual Score	Grand Total	Result	Indications
5 - 8	25 - 42	Low	Low scores indicate that you are not doing everything you can to maintain a high level personal wellness. The activities that follow will help you enhance your personal wellness.
9 - 11	43 - 60	Moderate	Moderate scores indicate that you are doing some of the things you need to do to maintain a high level personal wellness. The activities that follow will help you enhance your personal wellness.
12 - 15	61 - 75	High	High scores indicate that you are doing everything you can to maintain a high level personal wellness. The activities that follow will help you enhance your personal wellness even more.

Scale Descriptions

FP **FOOD PLAN** – People scoring High on this scale eat a healthy, well-balanced diet. They do not eat a lot of fast or processed foods, and eat lots of fruits and vegetables. They avoid sugars and fatty foods and eat healthy snacks.

S **SLEEP** – People scoring High on this scale get sufficient sleep to minimize stress that triggers thoughts, feelings and actions issues. They have a sleep routine, relax before going to bed, and avoid liquids, foods and substances that will keep them awake.

R **RELAXATION** – People scoring High on this scale are able to relax and enjoy life. They take walks, enjoy the outdoors, and engage in activities to unwind.

E **EXERCISE** – People scoring High on this scale engage in activities that allow them to remain physically healthy. They play sports and engage in aerobic exercises, strength training and flexibility training. They enjoy working outside for exercise.

SP **SOLVING PROBLEMS** – People scoring High on this scale are effective problem solvers. They are good at brainstorming solutions to their problems, making good decisions based on evidence and implementing their solutions.

Foods I Currently Eat

The more balanced and healthy your food plan, the less stress you will experience and the better you will feel. It can be eye-opening to journal about the foods you are currently eating.

Think about your current diet and the foods and liquids you consumed last week.

Day of the Week	Foods and Liquids I Consume	Healthier Foods and Liquids I Could Consume Instead
Monday		
Tuesday		
Wednesday		
Thursday		
Friday		
Saturday		
Sunday		

Dine Well?

Would Virginia Woolf think you *dined well?* Why or why not? Read her quotation below:

"One cannot think well, love well, sleep well, if one has not dined well."

With your lifestyle in mind, what is your definition of "thinking well"?

With your lifestyle in mind, what is your definition of "loving well"?

With your lifestyle in mind, what is your definition of "sleeping well"?

With your lifestyle in mind, what is your definition of "dining well"?

My Favorite Foods!

All people have favorite foods. Some of these foods are healthy and some are not.

In the spaces that follow, write about or draw four of your favorite foods, and describe why they are healthy or not healthy for you.

Food 1	Food 2
Food 3	Food 4

How can you make a promise to yourself to begin eating healthier foods?

____

____

____

What Do I Consume and Why?

Think about all of the different types of foods, liquids and substances you consume. List them, and describe why you think you consume them. They can be healthy or unhealthy.

☐ Fat

☐ Alcohol/Substances

☐ Caffeine

☐ Sugar in what you eat

☐ Sugar in what you drink

☐ Fruits

☐ Vegetables

(Continued on the next page)

What Do I Consume and Why? *(Continued)*

☐ Grains (rye, oats, wheat, etc.)

____

____

____

☐ Protein-rich foods

____

____

____

☐ Fish

____

____

____

☐ Fast/Processed foods

____

____

____

☐ Snacks

____

____

____

Which foods do you want to start eating more frequently?

____

____

____

Which foods do you want to stop eating so frequently?

____

____

____

Which foods do you feel you are eating in appropriate quantities?

____

____

____

My Sleep Routine

If you are experiencing thoughts, feelings and actions issues, you need to get adequate sleep each night. In order to do that, you also need to develop good sleep routines.
Think about the routine you have before going to bed each night.

In the spaces that follow each italicized tip, describe your sleep routine:

1) *Establish a time for going to bed and getting up in the morning*

Time I usually go to bed _______________ **Time I usually get up** _______________

2) *Avoid drinking before bedtime*

Before bed, I drink ____

3) *Avoid heavy eating after dinner*

Before bed, I eat ____

4) *Avoid naps during the daytime*

I take naps at: _______________ **For how long?** _______________

5) *Exercise early in the day*

My exercise early in the day is ______________________________________

6) *Avoid exercise or strenuous activities before bed*

My exercise or strenuous activities before bed ____________________________

____

7) *Wind down with quiet activities before getting into bed*

My quiet activities before bed include _________________________________

____

What do you need to change to improve your sleep routine?

____

____

____

My Sleep Diary

If you are experiencing sleep problems, you may have trouble figuring out what is keeping you from sleeping. If this is the case, you will definitely benefit from keeping a sleep diary. A sleep diary contains notes about your sleep habits.

Complete the following sleep diary information each night.

Day of the Week	Amount of Nap Time	Total Hours of Sleep at Night	Quality of Sleep 1 (not good) – 5 (great)	How Often I Awaken
Monday				
Tuesday				
Wednesday				
Thursday				
Friday				
Saturday				
Sunday				

On nights that you sleep well, what is different regarding your thoughts, feelings and actions?

____

On nights that you don't sleep well, what is different regarding your thoughts, feelings and actions?

____

____

Positive Leisure Time

People enjoy leisure time in different ways.
Some people like to spend leisure time with other people and some like to spend it alone.

Complete the table that follows to explore your favorite ways to spend leisure time.

Leisure Time	Activities I Enjoy	How They Help Me	Why I Don't Do More
Creative Activities			
Educational Activities			
Social Activities			
Solitary Activities			
Spiritual Activities			
Physical Activities			
Family/Community Activities			
Other			

What did you discover about your leisure time and how you benefit from the activities?

____

____

____

Unable to Relax?

For a variety of reasons, some people are unable to relax.

Complete the table that follows to explore the reasons you might not be able to relax.

Reasons I Cannot Relax	How It Hurts Me	What I Can Do About It
Example: Too Anxious	*I am constantly worried about something. I have panic attacks and painful symptoms.*	*I can meditate, stay-in-the-moment, be mindful, breathe deeply and adhere to The Serenity Prayer (Serenity to accept what cannot be changed, courage to change what I can and the wisdom to know the difference).*
Too Anxious		
Mood Changes		
Fear Recklessness		
Uncontrollable Anger		
Substance Abuse		
Other		
Other		

What did you learn about why you are unable relax?

____

____

____

RELAXATION

Relaxation is a part of everyone's lifestyle. It is important to take time to find ways to relax. The good news is that you can be creative and discover how to relax in many different ways.

Some of the calming activities that people engage in to relax:

- Take a walk in the woods
- Read a good book
- Talk with a friend
- Take a warm bath
- Do gentle stretching exercises
- Play with your pet

What are some of the things you can do, or would like to begin doing, to relax? You can use any of the above examples or create your own.

Things I Can Do to Relax	How the Activity Helps Me	How I Can Engage in this Activity More Often

Reducing Stress

Stress can intensify unwanted thoughts, feelings and actions issues. Following are some useful stress-management techniques.

Complete this table to identify effective stress-management techniques. Use Name Codes.

Aspects of My Lifestyle	Tried and Liked It. Why Do You Like It?	Have Not Tried It. Why Haven't You?	Tried and Do Not Like it. Why Not?
Relaxation – *Find a quiet place to relax, meditate, do yoga, listen to soothing music, follow some guided imagery, draw, write, breathe deeply.*			
Exercise – *Plan regular exercise, physical activity like sports, walking, jogging, aerobic exercising, yoga, martial arts.*			
Sleep – *Before bed, have a nighttime sleep routine: avoid heavy eating, drinking, and physical activity. Make sure the room conditions are comfortable.*			
Nutrition – *Eat nutritional well-balanced meals, which enhance your ability to be calm and stress-free.*			
Social Support – *Confide in and talk with trusted friends and family about your challenges.*			
Humor – *Tell and enjoy appropriate jokes, relay funny stories to others, watch humorous TV shows or movies.*			
Other			

Let's Get Physical

Exercise is important for everyone to be able to live a healthy, stress-free lifestyle. However, many people neglect this important aspect of staying healthy.

Identify how you like to stay physically active and how it helps you.

Physical Activity	How Much Time Devoted Per Week	How This Helps Me	If I Don't, Why Not?
Aerobic Exercise			
Bicycle			
Walk / jog / hike			
Play sports			
Aquatic Exercises			
Yoga, Tai Chi, etc.			
House work			
Yard work			
Garden			
Swim			
Rock Climb			
Stairs			
Weights			
Other			
Other			
Other			
Other			

Go back to the list and put a check by the activities you are willing to do more regularly.

Problem Solving - I

All people face problems in their personal and professional lives. Some of these problems seem insignificant, and others seem overwhelming. Worrying about your problems will not only fail to solve them, but it will also create additional stress. It is important to develop a system for solving the small or large problems you encounter in life.

Identify a problem you have encountered in life ______________________________

____

____

What are the elements of the problem? Who is involved? What happened? ______________

____

____

What are three possible solutions to your problem? Don't evaluate, just write your ideas down.

a) ____

____

b) ____

____

c) ____

____

Answer the following questions which correspond to your possible solutions above.
What is required to implement the solution?

a) ____

____

b) ____

____

c) ____

____

Do you have the time, money and skills to carry the solution out?

a) ____
b) ____
c) ____

Can the solution be implemented?

a) ____
b) ____
c) ____

Would the people involved be cooperative?

a) ____
b) ____
c) ____

(Continued on the next page)

Problem Solving - II *(Continued)*

Which solution provides you with the best chance of success? Why this solution?

____

____

____

How will you implement this solution? Break the solution down into manageable and achievable steps. What would the steps you need to take to implement your solution?

Step 1: ________________________________

Step 2: ________________________________

Step 3: ________________________________

Step 4: ________________________________

Step 5: ________________________________

What potential difficulties do you expect in implementing your solution?

Difficulty 1:______________________________

How will you handle it? ________________________

Difficulty 2:______________________________

How will you handle it? ________________________

Difficulty 3:______________________________

How will you handle it? ________________________

How did the solution work? ______________________

____

____

Did you resolve your problem, or do you need to implement another solution? ____________

____

____

____

____

This problem-solving method can be used with all of your problems!

(Continued on the next page)

Problem Solving – III *(Continued)*

Preparation

People who are prepared tend to feel less stress. By being prepared, you will be able to manage your stress much more effectively. By preparing for a stressful event, you will be able to manage whatever happens in the situation. Think about a stressful situation you have coming up. This might be a presentation at work, going to a party, changing jobs, etc.

What is a stressful situation you have coming up in the near future? ______________________

____

____

____

What steps can you take to prepare for the situation?

Step 1: How can I choose to *think* about it? ______________________________

____

Step 2: How can I choose to *feel* about it? ______________________________

____

Step 3: What is my *action* plan? ______________________________

____

Step 4: How do I visualize myself carrying out the plan? ______________________________

____

Step 5: How do I anticipate rewarding my positive actions? ______________________________

____

Now, you can rehearse the situation in your mind or out loud with a partner. Think about the situation, and go over in your mind what you think you will say or do in the situation.

Things I will say: ____

____

Things I will do: ____

____

"To Keep the Body in Good Health ..."

To keep the body in good health is a duty ... otherwise we shall not be able to keep our mind strong and clear.
~ Buddha

Write your thoughts about this quotation. Do you agree or disagree with the Buddha? How do you view the correlation between keeping your body in good health and keeping your mind strong and clear? Explain.

What are you doing to keep your body in good health?

What more could you be doing?

What are you doing to keep your mind strong and clear?

What more could you be doing?

MODULE IV

Possibilities

Trust yourself. Create the kind of self that you will be happy to live with all your life. Make the most of yourself by fanning the sparks of possibility into flames of achievement.

~ Golda Meir

Name ____

Date ______________________

Skills Emphasized in Each Activity Handout

Spare Time Activity Scheduling .... page 88
List five activities one has done in the past and would like to try in the future; note meaningful aspects of each; identify what has limited one's involvement in these activities and ways to increase or begin participation in them.

Social Isolation .... page 89
Complete six sentence starters highlighting the effects of unwanted thoughts, feelings and actions on social and recreational activities; identify reasons one isolates and read about the benefits of social support.

Breaking the Ice .... page 90
Practice starting and participating in a conversation; note the results of one's introduction, compliments, closed and open-ended questions, active listening and personal disclosure.

Making Friends .... page 92
Practice and journal about the results of reaching out, self-disclosure, showing interest and respect, valuing differences and developing trust.

Maintaining Friends .... page 93
Practice and journal about the results of meeting people with similar interests and planning related activities, disclosing feelings, asking appropriate details about the person's life and maintaining contact.

Everywhere are Signs .... page 94
Identify the early signs of experiencing up to eighteen specific symptoms; describe the difference between one's usual behavior and one's behavior when unwanted thoughts, feelings and actions occur.

Possibilities in My Life .... page 96
State possibilities related to areas of one's life; describe actions to make them happen and ways to pursue one's most important possibility.

I Have Dreams .... page 97
Read a quotation about stolen dreams, anger, grief, healing and restoration; personalize its message by answering five questions and stating what to do to achieve one's dream.

Cue Recognition .... page 98
Complete a checklist addressing nine indications of problems with recognizing social cues; read five tips for cue recognition; note situations that cause the most difficulty and other people's emotions that one finds hard to understand.

Set Long-Term Goals .... page 99
Document six long term goals, how they will improve one's life and what it takes to accomplish them.

Next, Set Short-Term Goals .... page 100
List short term task-oriented goals for each of six long term goals, how they will improve one's life and steps to accomplish them; prioritize by stating which goal one will work on first.

My Optimistic Future .... page 101
Demonstrate visualization by depicting and/or describing one's future regarding home life, making a living, positive thoughts, feelings and actions, and lifestyle.

Work Satisfaction .... page 102
Analyze one's work situation by describing at least six specific aspects; note the difficulties and ways to overcome them; state what one enjoys and how to make the most of the situations.

Managing My Unwanted Thoughts, Feelings and Actions at Work .... page 103
Review ten tips, select ones to implement immediately and identify how to accomplish them; answer questions about comparing oneself to others and ways to break seemingly overwhelming tasks into smaller steps.

My Dream Job .... page 104
Identify the concept of "daring to dream"!

Possibilities Scale
Introduction and Directions

Even though people may be struggling to control unwanted thoughts, feelings and actions, life is still full of many possibilities. The good news is that you can still have a very fulfilling life with loving relationships, a successful career and good times with your family.

This assessment contains 20 statements designed to help you explore how your thoughts, feelings and actions issues may be limiting the possibilities in your life. Read each of the statements and decide how descriptive the statement is of you. Circle the number under the column that describes how much that statement is like you.

In the following example, the circled 1 indicates the statement does not describe the person completing the inventory:

	A LOT	SOMETIMES	A LITTLE/NONE
I have stopped getting together with friends	(3)	2	1

This is not a test. Since there are no right or wrong answers, do not spend too much time thinking about your answers. Be sure to respond to every statement.

Turn to the next page and begin.

Possibilities Scale

	A LOT	SOMETIMES	A LITTLE/NONE
I have stopped getting together with friends	3	2	1
I am unable to motivate myself	3	2	1
I have stopped doing things I used to enjoy	3	2	1
I have no desire to leave the house	3	2	1
I still engage in hobbies I enjoy	1	2	3

ST - TOTAL = ________________

I have trouble starting conversations	3	2	1
I give compliments to other people	1	2	3
I don't listen well when others are speaking	3	2	1
I can't say no when asked to do something I don't want to do	3	2	1
I have trouble accepting criticism	3	2	1

S - TOTAL = ________________

I feel anxious when I think about the future	3	2	1
I am too unsure of myself to achieve anything	3	2	1
I feel like I can accomplish anything I want	1	2	3
I can't seem to get started in reaching my goals	3	2	1
I don't plan or structure my tasks	3	2	1

GO - TOTAL = ________________

I have a job and do it well	1	2	3
I don't trust my boss and/or co-workers	3	2	1
It's hard for me to concentrate on a job	3	2	1
I get flustered easily at work	3	2	1
I have good job-related skills	1	2	3

CO - TOTAL = ________________

Possibilities Scale Scoring Directions

The Possibilities Scale you just completed is designed to measure the possibilities in your life. For each of the sections on the previous page, count the scores you circled. Put that total on the line marked TOTAL at the end of each section.

Then, transfer your total to the space below:

ST = Spare-Time Possibilities TOTAL ___________

S = Social Possibilities TOTAL ___________

GO = Goal-Oriented Possibilities TOTAL ___________

CO = Career-Oriented Possibilities TOTAL ___________

Add your four scores together for your GRAND TOTAL ___________

Profile Interpretation

Individual Score	Grand Total	Result	Indications
5 - 8	20 - 33	Low	Low scores indicate that you are open to possibilities and not being held back by your unwanted thoughts, feelings and/ or actions. Complete the following exercises to reduce the effects even more.
9 - 11	34 - 46	Moderate	Moderate scores indicate that you are being somewhat open to possibilities and not being held back too much by your unwanted thoughts, feelings and/or actions. Complete the following exercises to learn to reduce the effects.
12 - 15	47 - 60	High	High scores indicate that you are not open to possibilities and you are held back by your unwanted thoughts, feelings and/or actions. Complete the following exercises to seriously reduce the effects.

Scale Descriptions

ST - SPARE-TIME POSSIBILITIES– People scoring high on this scale have stopped engaging in many of their favorite spare-time activities. They no longer go out with friends and have a hard time motivating themselves to be involved in their favorite leisure activities.

S - SOCIAL POSSIBILITIES – People scoring high on this scale tend to have difficulties developing and maintaining social relationships. They have a difficult time meeting new people, starting conversations, and listening attentively.

GO - GOAL-ORIENTED POSSIBILITIES – People scoring high on this scale tend to have difficulties in setting and reaching personal and professional goals. They cannot remain on task and get too anxious to accomplish their goals.

CO - CAREER-ORIENTED POSSIBILITIES – People scoring high on this scale tend to not have a job, or are not successful at the job. They may not trust the people with whom they work, or they may confuse work-related tasks.

GRAND TOTAL – High scores on all four scales indicate that the person is being held back by unwanted thoughts, feelings and/or actions issues and not open to possibilities. The following pages will be helpful to everyone, no matter how they scored.

Spare -Time Activity Scheduling

It is extremely important to make an effort to fill your free time with meaningful activities.

For this exercise, record your activities from last week, to develop a baseline. Next, think about ways that you can take part in these activities more often.

An Activity I Enjoy or have Enjoyed in the Past	This is Meaningful about this Activity	How I Can Engage in this Activity More Often

What is keeping you from engaging in your favorite activities?

____

____

Sometimes there are activities that look appealing to you, but you have not tried them.

For this exercise, record the activities you would like to try, why they are of interest, and how you can start to add them to your schedule.

An Activity I Want to Try	Why I Think it Would be Meaningful	How I Can Begin

What has kept you from engaging in these activities?

____

____

Social Isolation

You don't need to feel self-conscious, embarrassed and/or ashamed, and feel you have to hide away because you experience unwanted thoughts, feelings and/or actions. You need to do just the opposite. By staying connected to other people, you will experience less stress, find people who can support you, and have more fun.

Think about the following sentence starters as they relate to your participation in social and recreational activities. USE NAME CODES.

When I feel self-conscious, embarrassed and/or ashamed, I want to be by myself because

____

____

When I feel self-conscious, embarrassed and/or ashamed, I don't feel like being sociable, so I

____

____

____

When I feel self-conscious, embarrassed and/or ashamed, I miss taking part in social and recreational activities such as ______________________________

____

____

When I feel self-conscious, embarrassed and/or ashamed, I feel bad later because I missed out on

____

____

____

When I feel self-conscious, embarrassed and/or ashamed, I worry that I give others the impression that

____

____

____

I feel as if I am __________________________________

____

____

____

____

____

Breaking the Ice

Starting a conversation can be a difficult task, especially for people who experience unwanted thoughts, feelings and actions issues. Often, breaking the ice with people you do not know is the most difficult aspect of developing friendships.

Following is a system you can use for breaking the ice. Try it with a group member or with your counselor and then journal about your results.

- **Be the first to say hello.**
  What were the results?

- **Introduce yourself.**
  What were the results?

- **Provide a compliment along with an easy follow-up question.**

  What was the compliment and follow up question?

  What were the results?

- **Ask close-ended questions, questions that can be answered with a yes or no, never or always, one or two words ... a response that has nothing to build on.**
  Examples: How long have you lived here? (6 months)
  Where were you born? (Cleveland, Ohio)
  In this your first time here? (yes)

  What questions did you ask?

  What were the results?

(Continued on the next page)

Breaking the Ice *(Continued)*

- **Follow closed-ended questions with open-ended questions, questions that begin with who, where, what, when, why, how and/or who said?**

  Examples:
  - *How long have you lived here? Why did you move here?*
  - *Where were you born? How did you get involved in the work do you do?*
  - *Is this your first time here? What do you do when you are not working?*

  What questions did you ask?

  What were the results?

  When conversing, use examples from your past.

  What examples did you use?

  What were the results?

  Listen actively to what others say.

  How did you listen actively?

  What were the results?

  Respond by disclosing specific information related to the topic.

  What were the results?

  What were the results of your conversation?

Making Friends

Once you have started a conversation with new people, you can usually tell if the person has interests and values compatible with yours. If you want to begin developing a friendship with the person, try the following system for making friends.

Plan it, try it and then journal about the results.

Reach out to others.

How will you reach out? ______________________________

How did you reach out? ______________________________

What were the results? ______________________________

Self-disclose specific and appropriate information relevant to topics of conversation.

What might you disclose? ______________________________

What information did you disclose? ______________________________

What were the results? ______________________________

Show genuine interest in others.

How will you show interest in others? ______________________________

What did you do? ______________________________

What were the results? ______________________________

Treat others with respect.

How will you show respect? ______________________________

How did you do this? ______________________________

What were the results? ______________________________

Value the differences in others.

How will you value differences? ______________________________

What difference(s) did you value? ______________________________

How were you different? ______________________________

Develop trust.

How will you develop trust? ______________________________

How did you attempt this? ______________________________

What were the results? ______________________________

Maintaining Friends

After you have made friends, it is important to work at building and maintaining your friendships.

If you want to do so, try the following system and then journal about your results.

Meet people who have similar interests as you.

What are your interests?

Where can you meet people of the same interests?

Develop trust by disclosing specific and appropriate feelings.

How did you do this?

Ask appropriate details about the person's life.

What did you discover?

Plan activities around mutual interests.

What types of activities would this be?

Continue to maintain contact with these people.

How will you do this?

Everywhere Are Signs

To be open to more possibilities, it is critical that you are able to identify the signs when you begin to experience unwanted thoughts, feelings and actions issues.

Below, explore how you usually feel and then how you feel when you are beginning to experience a disturbance. If the symptom is not applicable to you, write n/a.

Symptom	How I Usually Behave	How I Behave When I Start Having Unwanted Thoughts, Feelings and Actions
Example: *Disorganized speech*	*I am able to organize my thoughts and speech.*	*I speak incoherently because I can't organize my thoughts.*
Disorganized speech		
Loss of interest in hygiene		
Magical thinking		
Reduced emotional expression		
Decreased motivation		
Decline in functioning		
Ability to concentrate		
Inability to handle daily hassles		

(Continued on the next page)

Everywhere Are Signs *(Continued)*

Symptom	How I Usually Behave	How I Behave When I Start Having Unwanted Thoughts, Feelings and Actions
Anxiety		
Hallucinations		
Delusions		
Thoughts about suicide		
Unusual thoughts		
Suspicious of others		
Withdrawing from friends		
Sleep changes		
Managing stress		
Other ____________		

Possibilities in My Life

People with unwanted thoughts, feelings and actions issues often find it difficult to see the possibilities in their lives. They can only see the negative side of their situation and they are unable to be positive. Now is the time to explore the possibilities in the various areas of your life.

In the table below discuss the possibilities you have in the major areas of your life.

Areas of My Life	The Possibilities I Have	What I Need to do to Make It Happen
Family	*Have a close family, celebrate occasions, enjoy each other.*	*Be a more consistent family member, caring person, and someone my family wants to be with.*
Family		
School		
Friends		
Dating Relationships		
Work/Career		
Neighbors Community		
Other		

What is the most important possibility you want to pursue? How will you do so?

___

___

___

I Have Dreams

Someone may have stolen your dream when it was young and fresh and you were innocent. Anger is natural. Grief is appropriate. Healing is mandatory. Restoration is possible.

~Jane Rubietta

What does this quote mean to you? ______________________________

____

____

____

How did you feel when reading this quote? ______________________________

____

____

____

What dreams have been stolen from you? ______________________________

____

____

____

____

What dreams do you now have? ______________________________

____

____

____

What do you need to do to achieve these dreams? ______________________________

____

____

____

____

____

If you are willing, share your dreams with others in the room.

Cue Recognition

Recognizing social cues (cue recognition) is important in all social interactions. People with unwanted thoughts, feelings and actions issues often have difficulty reading other people's cues in social situations, conversations or relationships.

Some of the following could indicate problems with recognizing social cues.
Check any that apply to you.

- ☐ I have trouble reading social cues. (e.g., facial expressions, gestures, tone of voice)
- ☐ I misinterpret what people say.
- ☐ I am easily manipulated by others.
- ☐ I have difficulty telling the difference between playful and mean-spirited teasing.
- ☐ I have difficulty guessing what other people may be thinking.
- ☐ I have trouble knowing when people are joking or if they actually mean it.
- ☐ I jump to conclusions about a social interaction.
- ☐ I have difficulty figuring out what other people will do or how they might react.
- ☐ I have trouble explaining things in a way that other people can understand.

Tips for Successful Cue Recognition

- If you don't understand what someone is saying, ask the person to clarify the meaning.
- Use paraphrasing or use your own words to restate what you believe the other person has said so that the person can correct you if needed ("So what you are saying is ...").
- Ask a friend or someone you trust to give you a second opinion about a confusing situation.
- Ask people you trust to suggest ways to deal with situations in which a misunderstanding has occurred.
- Keep track of the kinds of social situations in which you experience problems or misunderstandings.

Which situations cause you the most difficulty?

____

____

____

What feelings or emotions by others are hard for you to understand?

____

____

____

Set Long-Term Goals

Goals are important to help you achieve what you desire in life. They promote the notion that you have control over what happens in your future. Goals are those things you would like to obtain or accomplish. It is best to first set long-term goals that may take months or years to accomplish and then set short-term goals – steps to achieve those goals.

In the table that follows list long-term goals you would like to accomplish and how these accomplishments will make your life better and what it will take to accomplish them.

Things I Would Like to Accomplish in the Next Months or Years	How This Will Make My Life Better	What it Will Take to Accomplish it
Example: Move from my apartment	*Better public transportation, safer, closer to family, close to work so I can get there on time.*	*Get my finances in order.*
1.		
2.		
3.		
4.		
5.		
6.		

Follow this handout with *Next, Set Short-Term Goals*

Next, Set Short-Term Goals

In the table that follows (after you have completed the handout Set Long-Term Goals) list the short-term goals from your long-term goals which you listed, how they will make your life better and the steps you will take to accomplish them.
You may be able to start today!

Short-Term Goals I Have for the Future	How These Short-Term Goals Will Make My Life Better	Steps I Will Take to Accomplish Them
Example: Go the bank. Talk to my brother about where to move. Line people up to help me.	*It helps me to prioritize, have a plan, and look forward to moving and a better life.*	*Thursday I will go to the bank. Call my brother and make a date to have dinner with him next week. Talk to a few friends and ask if they'll help me move when I'm ready.*
1.		
2.		
3.		
4.		
5.		
6.		

Which goal will you start working on first? ______________________________

____

My Optimistic Future

Successful people are able to visualize their future and take small steps in order to reach their ultimate goals. They project their will into the future in order to create a series of events that lead to a better life. They then work to make this future a reality. What is your vision for your future? Think about what you want your life to be like in ten years.

In the spaces that follow, write about or draw your vision of your future in terms of your lifestyle.

What will your home life be like?	How will you earn a living?
Describe your positive thoughts.	Describe what your positive feelings will be.
Describe what your positive actions will be.	Describe your lifestyle.

Work Satisfaction

In the spaces in the first table, describe your current work situation, your difficulties and how you can overcome these difficulties. In the spaces in the second table below, describe your current work situation, what you enjoy and how you can make the most of the situations.

My Current Work Situation	My Difficulties	How I Can Overcome Them
The work I do		
Where I am working		
My supervisor		
My co-workers		
The type of work I am doing		
How I am using my interests and skills		
Others		

My Current Work Situation	What I Enjoy About it	How I Can Make the Most of It
The work I do		
Where I am working		
My supervisor		
My co-workers		
The type of work I am doing		
How I am using my interests and skills		
Others		

Managing My Unwanted Thoughts, Feelings and Actions at Work

Coping with unwanted thoughts, feelings and actions at work can be made easier by taking care of yourself in the workplace.

TIPS

- Learn techniques for staying calm and stress-free in the workplace.
- Take time off if needed.
- Don't compare yourself to others.
- If you take doctor's prescribed medication, take it consistently, as prescribed.
- Break tasks into small steps to avoid feeling overwhelmed.
- Take breaks when they are available to you.
- Have a quiet place to work, if possible.
- Talk to your supervisor about your needs.
- Don't let your work become your life.
- Use the Employee Assistance Program (if available).

Which of the tips will you be able to implement immediately? How will you do so?

____

____

____

To whom do you compare yourself? Why?

____

____

____

What types of tasks are you given that seem overwhelming?

____

____

____

How could you break these tasks down into smaller steps so you are not so overwhelmed?

____

____

____

My Dream Job

Write an advertisement for your dream job.

Explain your qualifications and/or your plan to develop the required skills

MODULE V

Erasing the Stigma of Mental Health Issues

We live in a time when the words impossible and unsolvable are no longer part of the scientific community's vocabulary. Each day we move closer to trials that will not just minimize the symptoms of disease and injury but eliminate them.

~ Christopher Reeve

Name ______________________________

Date______________________

Erasing the Stigma of Mental Health Issues Introduction

A stigma is extreme social disapproval of some type of personal characteristic or a belief that is not considered *socially acceptable*. People who have a particular attribute considered unwanted by society are rejected or stigmatized as a result of that attribute. People who experience unwanted thoughts, feelings and actions, are often judged unfairly to be crazy, violent, unpredictable, explosive, aggressive and/or unstable. These judgments, or social stigmas, can cause people who experience these issues to feel devalued as human beings. They are often ostracized from activities, rejected in social situations, stereotyped, minimized in the workplace, and shunned by others. People experiencing the stigma of unwanted thoughts, feelings and actions issues often feel extreme physical and psychological distress.

People who stigmatize and/or stereotype others bring about unfair treatment rather than help. This unfair treatment can be very obvious. For example, people make negative comments or laugh. On the other hand, this unfair treatment can be very subtle. For example, people assume that a person who experiences unwanted thoughts, feelings and actions issues is dangerous or violent, and they avoid or shun that person.

Stigmas affect a large percentage of people throughout the world. Some of the more common stigmas are associated with physical disabilities, mental health issues, age, body type, gender, sexual orientation, nationality, religion, family, ethnicity, race, religion, financial status, social sub-cultures and conduct. Stigmas set people apart from society and produce feelings in them of shame and isolation. People who are stigmatized are often considered socially unacceptable and they suffer prejudice, rejection, avoidance and discrimination.

WHAT CAN BE DONE?

Fear of judgment and ridicule about unwanted thoughts, feelings and actions often compels individuals and their families to hide from society rather than face criticism, shunning, labeling and stereotyping. Instead of seeking treatment, they struggle in silence. Let's discuss some ways you can combat the stereotypes and stigmas that are associated with these issues.

- You and your loved ones have choices. You can decide who is to know about your unwanted thoughts, feelings and actions, and what to tell them. You need not feel ashamed or embarrassed.
- You are not alone. Remember that many other people are coping with a similar situation.
- Look into or start a support group to meet others who experience what you do.
- Seek help and remember that the activities in this book and treatment from medical professionals can help you to have a productive education and career, and live satisfying lives.
- Be proactive and surround yourself with supportive people – people you can trust. Social isolation is a negative side effect of the stigma linked to unwanted thoughts, feelings and actions issues. Isolating yourself and discontinuing enjoyable activities will not help.

HOW CAN THIS MODULE HELP ME?

Managing Unwanted Thoughts, Feelings and Actions Workbook is designed to help you deal more effectively with your issues, and this section is specifically designed to help you overcome the stigma attached to those issues. Complete the activities that follow to feel better about yourself, feel content, and become more resilient in the face of stress in your life.

Skills Emphasized in Each Activity Handout

Two Types of Mental Health Stigma .... page 112
Read two definitions, describe relevant incidents one has experienced and differentiate whether each incident exemplifies social or perceived stigma.

The Stigma of Unwanted Thoughts, Feelings and Actions Issues THE PAST .... page 113
Document five or more people with whom one has discussed the issues, what was said, the persons' reactions, and how one felt; give an opinion regarding reasons for a negative reaction.

The Stigma of Unwanted Thoughts, Feelings and Actions Issues THE FUTURE .... page 114
List at least five supportive people, what one will say, the expected reactions and what could be gained or lost due to the discussions. Brainstorm with peers at what point in a serious relationship it is time to discuss one's issues.

Are You Ashamed? .... page 115
State one's personal application of a quotation from the "Stand Up for Mental Health" Campaign; explain its meaning and whether and why one is ashamed; write one's own story to inspire others.

If We Stamp Out the Stigma .... page 116
Journal thoughts about a quotation and identify ways to do one's part to erase the stigma of unwanted thoughts, feelings and actions issues.

Glenn Close Said ... . page 117
Read a quotation and answer twelve questions about ways to change one's own and others' views about mental health issues.

Effects of Unwanted Thoughts, Feelings and Actions Issues .... page 118
Read eight harmful effects of the stigma and describe whether and how one has been affected. Name support persons with whom one can discuss the effects and state reasons for choosing these people.

The Stigma of Going to a Mental Health Therapist .... page 119
Write one's prior ideas about therapy and then read sixteen facts about mental health and therapy. Identify which concepts were previously unknown and state one's concerns about seeking help. Consider the invitation to sign a commitment to speak to a therapist; sign if in agreement.

Stereotypes .... page 120
State ways one defies seven stereotypes of people with unwanted thoughts, feelings and actions issues. Document a message to people who label oneself.

Coping with the Stigma of Unwanted Thoughts, Feelings and Actions Issues .... page 121
Describe how one would educate others, with whom one would and would not share information and document one's knowledge about the issues. Name famous people with similar issues; identify one's special qualities and contributions to the world.

What Can You Do? .... page 122
List one's own and peers' ideas about ways to erase the stigma of mental health issues.

My Negative Thoughts .... page 123
Identify one's ideas about what others may think; complete six sentence starters and then place a large "X" over the misconceptions; practice visualizing the big "X" when negative thoughts occur.

Focus on Your Strengths .... page 124
Describe one's strengths related to community, relationships, work, creativity and special skills; identify ways to share these with others.

Skills Emphasized in Each Activity Handout *(Continued)*

Ways I Try to Minimize My Unwanted Thoughts, Feelings and Actions Issues .... page 125
Read six ways one may minimize the issues and give other examples; for each, identify the effects on oneself and others and better ways to cope.

Ways I Am Treated .... page 126
Give examples of ways one is treated by oneself and others by filling in eight text boxes in response to prompts.

Self-Doubt .... page 0127
Document five ways one doubts oneself, the effects and what one can do to control self doubt in positive and strong ways. Describe how a quotation about moving beyond self-doubt applies to oneself.

A Poster about the STIGMA of People with Unwanted Thoughts, Feelings and Actions Issues .... page 128
Depict and describe how one believes unwanted thoughts, feelings and actions issues look when being stigmatized by others.

A Poster about ACCEPTANCE of People with Unwanted Thoughts, Feelings and Actions Issues .... page 129
Depict and describe how one believes unwanted thoughts, feelings and actions issues look when being accepted by others.

DE-STIGMA-TIZE with the Facts about Mental Health Issues .... page 130
Read eight myths and eight facts that refute them; acknowledge the importance of participating in mental health treatment.

Coping with the Stigma of a Mental Health Issue .... page 131
In response to four suggestions, answer five questions to help oneself access treatment and workplace assistance, reduce self-doubt and shame, and replace isolation with supportive relationships. Share ideas with peers if willing.

Speak Out Against Stigmas .... page 132
Read about the methods and benefits of advocating for oneself and others; document responses to suggestions about events, publications, Internet and other opportunities to promote positive messages.

Two Types of Mental Health Stigma

Mental health stigma can be divided into two types:

1. **Social stigma** is characterized by prejudicial attitudes and discriminatory behavior directed towards individuals with mental health issues.
2. **Perceived stigma** is the internalizing by the people with mental health issues of their understanding of discrimination.

Name some incidents when you felt people were judging you, talking about you or discriminating against you because of your thoughts, feelings and actions issues. Next to your description of the incident, mark a number 1 or number 2, to indicate whether it was a social stigma or a perceived stigma. If you're not sure which, mark it with a question mark.

Often one perceives others' stigmatizing, or exaggerates others' or their own reactions.

The Stigma of Unwanted Thoughts, Feelings and Actions Issues – THE PAST

Experiencing unwanted thoughts, feelings and actions is becoming more commonplace in the world. Often the stigma attached to these issues stops one from moving forward - being unable to talk about it for fear of being judged or labeled. We can erase the stigma of any mental health issues by starting to discuss it with one person at a time, and taking the time to explain thoughts and feelings.

Let's start with whom you have already shared.

With whom have you discussed your issues?	What did you say?	What was this person's reaction? What did the person say?	How did you feel?
Family			
Friends			
Acquaintances			
Teachers, Coaches and/or Other School Administrators			
School Counselor and/or Mental Health Professional			
Other			

If any one of the above reacted in a negative way, to what do you attribute that reaction? ___________

____

____

____

The Stigma of Unwanted Thoughts, Feelings and Actions Issues – THE FUTURE

People often have perceptions about people who have thoughts, feelings and actions issues. One of the ways to erase this stigma is to talk about it and let others know that people who have these issues are just like anyone else who have some type of an issue.

Perhaps it is time to talk with other people whom you trust and/or with whom you feel safe.

Person with whom you might discuss your issue	What would you say to this person?	What do you think this person's reaction might be?	What could you gain and/or lose by discussing it with this person?
Family			
Friends			
Acquaintances			
Teachers, Coaches and/or Other School Administrators			
School Counselor and/or Mental Health Professional			
Other			

Brainstorm this with the group:

At what point, in a serious relationship, is it time to discuss your issues?

Are you Ashamed?

Don't be ashamed of your story. It will inspire others!

~ Healthyplace.com for the "Stand Up For Mental Health" Campaign

What does this quote mean to you? ______________________________

In what ways are you ashamed of your story? Why? ______________________________

Write about your story so it can inspire others.

My Story:

Use another sheet of paper to continue your story.

If We Stamp Out the Stigma ...

Journal your thoughts about the following quotation and describe how you can do your part to erase the stigma of unwanted thoughts, feelings and actions issues:

If we stamp out the stigma attached to mental health issues, shed the shame and eliminate the fear, then we open the door for people to speak freely about what they are feeling and thinking.

~ Jaletta Albright Desmond

Glenn Close said …

The most powerful way to change someone's view is to meet them … People who do come out and talk about mental illness, that's when healing can really begin. You can lead a productive life.

Name a time when you have changed someone else's view – about anything. ____________________

____

____

How did that feel to you? ____

____

____

Name a time you were tempted to talk about your unwanted thoughts, feelings and actions issues, but didn't. Why not?

____

____

Write about a situation in which you DID talk about your thoughts, feelings and actions issues.

____

____

How did that feel?____

How did it work out? ____

____

Who is a trusted person you can talk with and begin to heal yourself? ________________________

____

Anyone else?____

Who is a trusted person you can ask for a referral of someone to talk with in order to begin to heal?

____

____

Anyone else? ____

In an ideal world, how can you lead a more stable life?___________________________________

____

____

How can you contribute to changing stigma?____

____

____

Effects of Unwanted Thoughts, Feelings and Actions Issues

Check out these harmful effects of the stigma of thoughts, feelings and actions issues. Write on the lines next to each item if it has affected you in some way and how.

1. Lack of understanding by family ______________________________

   ____
2. Lack of understanding by friends ______________________________

   ____
3. Lack of understanding by teachers, coaches and/or other school administrators ______________

   ____
4. Discrimination at work ______________________________

   ____
5. Inability to join clubs or organizations ______________________________

   ____
6. Bullying; physical, emotional, verbal or sexual abuse or harassment ______________

   ____
7. Peer pressure from friends ______________________________

   ____
8. The belief that you will never be able to succeed or that you can't improve your situation.

   ____

   ____

On the line of the corresponding number, write the name of a person you can speak to, a person who might help to support you about each of the situations you noted above. Add a reason you've chosen that person.

1. ______________________________
2. ______________________________
3. ______________________________
4. ______________________________
5. ______________________________
6. ______________________________
7. ______________________________
8. ______________________________

The Stigma of Going to a Mental Health Therapist

Many people have pre-conceived ideas about anyone seeking therapy.

Write what you know about the experience.____

____

____

Here are some facts about mental health and mental health therapy.

- ☐ Mental health includes how you act, feel and think in different situations.
- ☐ Mental health problems can be caused by many different things including medical health issues, abuse (emotional, physical, verbal, sexual), stress, worry, loss of a relationship, food issues, self-injuries, ADHD, STD's, family changes, addictions, a traumatic event, problems, wanting to build up self-confidence, etc.
- ☐ If someone goes to a mental health therapist, this does NOT mean the person is crazy. Twenty percent of teens have mental health issues. Doctors and mental health therapists treat people the same as any other doctor treats problems (broken leg, diabetes, cancer, etc.).
- ☐ There needs to be a good connection between you and the therapist. Your therapist should be someone you feel you can trust.
- ☐ This might take a few meetings and/or a few therapists, to find the right one for you.
- ☐ Non-judgmental people who truly care about you will not judge you in a negative way. They will be proud of you for seeking help.
- ☐ The therapist does not assume that you have a mental illness. The therapist assumes something is troubling you, knows that no one leads a perfect life, and admires you for trying to make changes in your life.
- ☐ The therapist's job is to help you understand what's going on.
- ☐ The therapist will not tell you how to live your life, or how to think, act or believe.
- ☐ The therapist is not an advice-giver, but will help you think about how to increase your quality of life.
- ☐ The therapist may have some thoughts, and with you, will help you make changes.
- ☐ The therapist can help you to increase your life management skills.
- ☐ The therapist will help you recognize and express your feelings in a healthy way.
- ☐ The only person who can "fix" your problems is you, but a therapist will help you with an action plan.
- ☐ The mental health therapist may suggest that you see a medical doctor for medication.
- ☐ Therapy can be a slow or long process. Being open and honest, and wanting to feel better, will make the difference.

Place an X by the facts that you were not aware of.

What worries you about talking with a mental health therapist?

____

____

After learning about these facts, sign below if you will make a commitment to speak with a counselor or therapist.

Signature ________________________________ Date _______________

Stereotypes

The social stigmas about unwanted thoughts, feelings and actions issues often translate into the following inaccurate stereotypes.

In the table below, write about how you are unlike the stereotype provided.

Stereotype	How I Defy that Stereotype
They are all violent.	
They show no emotions.	
There is no such thing as a mental health issue.	
They see and hear things that aren't real.	
They have weird brains.	
They just pretend to have mental health issues.	
Other stereotypes of unwanted thoughts, feelings and actions issues.	

What would you like to say to other people who label you with these or other stereotypes?

____

____

____

Coping with the Stigma of Unwanted Thoughts, Feelings and Actions Issues

The stigma of having an issue such as unwanted thoughts, feelings and actions is often more damaging than the issue itself. Athough we have come a long way, the acceptance of mental health issues is still a long way off.

Learning to cope with your issue and the stigma that surrounds it will be helpful.

People treat you a bit differently. They might think of you as violent and explosive, not knowing what your mood might be like, and they might avoid you altogether. What can you do about that? Consider educating them about your issues. What could you say?

____

____

Use your own discretion. It is important for you and your well-being to be educated about your unwanted thoughts, feelings and actions issues and to decide whether, and with whom, to share and/or educate. Trust your instinct. Educate and share with others with whom you feel most comfortable and trust.

____

____

With whom are you comfortable to tell about your issue and why? ____________________

____

____

With whom are you *not* comfortable to tell about your issue and why? ________________

____

____

Own your condition. Learn how to educate yourself about it, manage it and cope with it.

What do you already know about it? ______________________________

____

Accept that you are special, worthwhile and have much to offer the world. Many famous people had the same condition *(example John Nash - movie "A Beautiful Mind" and Mary Todd Lincoln)*. What famous contemporary people have you read or heard about who have thoughts, feelings and actions issues?

____

____

Do not be defined by your issues. What is special about you and what do you have to offer to your self and to the world?

____

____

____

____

What can YOU Do?

Don't let what you cannot do interfere with what you can do.

~ John Wooden

How can YOU get the word out to erase the stigma of mental health issues?

Brainstorm with a few other people about how your group can get the word out to erase the stigma of mental health issues?

My Negative Thoughts

You can begin to overcome the stigma related to unwanted thoughts, feelings and actions issues by refusing to worry about what others think. When you are worried about what others say about you, or might say about you, you will have a difficult time enjoying life.

What are the negative thoughts that go through your head about others and what they think of you?

Others think I am …

Others don't think I can …

Others probably find me …

I think others might be afraid or wary of me because …

Others label me as …

This makes me feel …

Now that you have written these thoughts, take a big heavy black marker and put a big **X** through all of the thoughts above. When these negative thoughts come into your head, picture that big X, reminding you not to worry about what others think.

Focus on Your Strengths

You can do many things to help fight the stigma associated with your issue. You can focus on your strengths rather than your limitations. Demonstrate to others, and yourself, that you have a great deal to offer.

In the spaces that follow, identify some of your strengths. You have much to share, so take a few minutes to think about and write about some of your greatest strengths.

My strengths related to the community:

____

____

My strengths related to relationships with others:

____

____

My strengths related to my work or volunteer job:

____

____

My strengths related to creativity:

____

____

My strengths related to special skills I possess:

____

____

How can you share these strengths to show others that even though you may have your thoughts, feelings and action issues, you are a capable, talented human being?

____

____

Ways I Try to Minimize My Unwanted Thoughts, Feelings and Actions Issues

Many people dealing with unwanted thoughts, feelings and actions will try a variety of ways to minimize the stigma.

Complete the following table to explore the various ways that you minimize your issues and how this makes you feel. Describe some better ways to cope.

Ways I Minimize My Thoughts, Feelings And Actions	The Effect This Has on Me and Others	A Better way to Cope
Example: *I pretend that nothing is wrong with me.*	*Others think I'm just acting badly rather than thinking I have an actual mental health issue.*	*Apologize for my actions. Explain and say that I've been having some mental health issues and I'm working on them.*
I pretend that nothing is wrong with me.		
I refuse to get help.		
I say things like "Nothing can ever help me."		
I will not talk about my mental health issues.		
I laugh and make jokes about my actions.		
I avoid people.		
Other		

Ways I Am Treated

Think about some of the ways that people treat you because of your unwanted thoughts, feelings and actions. In the spaces below, explore the various ways people treat you. Write about those who treat you unfairly and why.

I am rejected by family … *(example: RGT calls me names.)*

I am rejected by my friends …

I encounter problems at work …

I encounter problems at home …

I am subjected to physical violence or harassment …

I am laughed at …

I treat myself unfairly by …

I treat myself fairly by …

Self-Doubt

Don't let stigma create self-doubt and shame. One of the most important ways to minimize the stigma of unwanted thoughts, feelings and actions issues is to explore how one doubts oneself. Self-doubt almost always stems from a lack of understanding rather than information based on the facts. Feeling ashamed, embarrassed or humiliated because of a mental health issue can be self-defeating.

How do your unwanted thoughts, feelings and actions issues cause you to doubt yourself and how can you control your self-doubt in a positive and strong way?

Ways I Doubt Myself	How This Negatively Affects Me	What I Can Do About it

However you arrive at the ability to ignore self-doubt - if you can acquire it or possess it or find it or discover it – move beyond self-doubt.

~ Dwight Yoakum

How do you relate to this quotation? ______________________________

____

____

A Poster about the STIGMA of People with Unwanted Thoughts, Feelings and Actions Issues

In the space that follows, draw a collage of pictures, symbols and/or words, of how you believe unwanted thoughts, feelings and actions issues look when people are being stigmatized by others.

A Poster about ACCEPTANCE of People with Unwanted Thoughts, Feelings and Actions Issues

In the space that follows, draw a collage of pictures, symbols and/or words, of how you believe unwanted thoughts, feelings and actions issues look, when people are accepted.

DE-STIGMA-TIZE with the Facts about Mental Health Issues

Myth: Mental health issues are rare.

Fact: Mental health issues are not rare and affect nearly everyone either directly or indirectly.

Myth: People with mental health issues are unable to lead successful, productive lives.

Fact: Most people with a mental health issue respond to treatment, learn to cope with and manage their problems, and go on to lead productive and fulfilling lives.

Myth: People who have mental health issues will not get better.

Fact: Once diagnosed, mental health issues are treatable. While they are not always cured, they can be managed effectively. Most people with mental health issues live productive and positive lives while receiving treatments for their mental health issues. As is the case with any mental health issues, individuals with severe or persistent mental health issues who respond poorly to available treatments may require more support and may not function as highly as others.

Myth: People with mental health issues are violent and unpredictable.

Fact: While some people who suffer from mental health issues do commit antisocial acts, it does not equal criminality or violence - despite the media's tendency to emphasize a suspected link. People with mental health issues are no more likely to commit violence than anyone in the general public, but they are more likely to be victimized and are more likely to inflict violent behaviors on themselves.

Myth: Mental health issues happen because of bad parenting or personal weakness.

Fact: The main risk factors for mental health issues are not bad parenting or personal weakness but rather genetics, severe and prolonged stress (such as physical or sexual abuse), or other environmental influences (such as birth trauma or head injury).

Myth: Treatment for mental health issues is not usually effective.

Fact: The effectiveness of any treatment depends on a number of factors including the type of mental health issue and the particular needs of the individual. A combination of psychiatric medication and psychotherapy, or social interventions are the most effective way to treat mental health issues.

Myth: Mental health issues are caused by everyday stressors.

Fact: It may seem that stress is responsible for mental health issues; however, there is no one clear cause of these issues. Rather, it is a result of complex interactions between psychological, biological, genetic and social factors. Stress, stigma, and lack of support can make it worse on the individual.

Myth: Mental health issues are always hereditary.

Fact: Some mental health issues include a genetic component, which results in a predisposition or vulnerability toward the illness among children and siblings, but environment also plays a key role in the development of certain mental health issues. If someone in a person's family has a mental health issue, that person will be at higher risk.

If you start to experience the symptoms of a mental health issue, it is important for you to see a medical professional to determine if you have a problem that will require treatment. If you know of anyone who seems to have symptoms of a mental health issue, urge that person to do the same.

Coping with the Stigma of a Mental Health Issue

Get treatment. Don't let the fear of being labeled with a mental health issue prevent you from seeking help. Treatment can provide relief by identifying and reducing symptoms that interfere with your work and personal life. How can you get treatment?

____

____

____

____

Don't let stigma create self-doubt and shame. If you are buying into the stigma, you will have the mistaken belief that your issue is a sign of personal weakness, or that you should be able to control it better. How can you have less self-doubt?

____

____

____

____

How can you have less shame?______________________

____

____

____

____

Don't isolate yourself. Have the courage to confide in your family members, friends, dating partner, clergy, school counselor or other members of your groups and/or community. Who can you reach out to and who can you trust for the compassion, support and understanding you need?

____

____

____

____

Get help at work. If you are having unwanted thoughts, feelings and actions issues that affect your work, confidentially talk with your supervisor, explain what you are doing to help yourself, and find out what plans and programs are available might help.

____

____

____

If you and others are willing, share responses.

Speak Out Against Stigmas

It can help instill courage in others who are facing unwanted thoughts, feelings and actions issues, it will help to educate the public about the effect that these issues have on you personally. Speaking out for, and about yourself, advocates for others who might have these issues and it can be beneficial to you at the same time.

Think about some of the ways that you might let your voice be heard about stigmas and their damaging effects on people. For each of the items, list the ways that you could speak out against stigmas.

Express your opinions at events. What events are planned in your place of employment where you might speak out against stigmas?

____

____

____

At what events in your community might you volunteer to speak out against stigmas?

____

____

____

You could write an informative feature article or letter to the editor of a local newspaper or your school newspaper. What would you say?

____

____

____

You could blog about stigmas on the Internet. How can you do this? ____________________

____

____

What are some other ways to speak out against stigmas? ____________________

____

____

How do you think this will benefit others?____________________

____

____

How will it benefit you? ____________________

____

____